Increasing Student Learning Through Multimedia Projects

ASCD

Association for Supervision and Curriculum Development

Alexandria, Virginia USA

Michael Simkins
Karen Cole
Fern Tavalin
Barbara Means

Association for Supervision and Curriculum Development
1703 N. Beauregard St. • Alexandria, VA 22311-1714 USA
Telephone: 1-800-933-2723 or 703-578-9600 • Fax: 703-575-5400
Web site: http://www.ascd.org • E-mail: member@ascd.org

2002–2003 ASCD Executive Council: Peyton Williams Jr. (*President*),
Raymond J. McNulty, (*President-Elect*), Kay A. Musgrove, (*Immediate
Past President*), Pat Ashcraft, Martha Bruckner, Mary Ellen Freeley,
Richard L. Hanzelka, Douglas E. Harris, Mildred Huey, Susan Kerns,
Robert Nicely Jr., James Tayler, Andrew Tolbert, Sandra K. Wegner,
Jill Dorler Wilson.

The contents of this book were developed under a Technology Innovation Challenge Grant from the Department of Education. The contents
do not necessarily represent the policy of the Department of Education
and do not assume endorsement by the Federal Government.

Cover art copyright © 2002 by ASCD.

All Web links in this book are correct as of the publication date
below but may have become inactive or otherwise modified since
that time. If you notice a deactivated or changed link, please e-mail
books@ascd.org with the words "Link Update" in the subject line. In
your message, please specify the Web link, the book title, and the
page number on which the link appears.

Printed in the United States of America.

September 2002 member book (pcr). ASCD Premium, Comprehen-
sive, and Regular members periodically receive ASCD books as part
of their membership benefits. No. FY03-01.

ASCD Product No. 102112

ASCD member price: $17.95   nonmember price: $21.95

Library of Congress Cataloging-in-Publication Data

Increasing student learning through multimedia projects / Michael
Simkins ... (et al.).
      p.   cm.
Includes bibliographical references and index.
"ASCD Product No. 102112"—T.p. verso.
   ISBN 0-87120-664-1 (alk. paper)
   1. Media programs (Education)—United States. 2. Interactive
multimedia—United States 3. Project method in teaching—United
States. I. Simkins, Michael, 1948–
   LB1028.4   .I53 2002
   371.33'5—dc21

                                        2002007798

07 06 05 04 03 02   10 9 8 7 6 5 4 3 2 1

Increasing Student Learning Through Multimedia Projects

Foreword

Project-based-learning classrooms are abuzz with productive discussion and the excitement of learning. Students are investigating rich and challenging topics, from the Civil War to the drug war, in the context of real-world issues and data. Their studies seamlessly integrate science, mathematics, English, history, politics, and the arts. Project work is group work, with students questioning, discussing, and probing each other's opinions.

In addition to the teacher, other adults—parents, business and community volunteers, student teachers, and teacher's aides—are also in the room assisting student teams. The teams have access to multimedia technology of various kinds, enabling them to access worlds of knowledge beyond the classroom, consult with other experts, assemble their work, and share it with their teachers and classmates. They know that the audience for their ideas lies beyond their classrooms—in their families, the community, and visitors to their Web sites.

This portrait of a different kind of classroom illustrates how project-based learning is much more than a "classroom strategy" or a "textbook supplement." When fully realized, project-based learning can be the foundation for transforming schools and, together with intelligent use of technology, can create the kind of Digital-Age education our students deserve.

Project-based learning redefines the boundaries of the classroom. No longer are students confined to learning within four walls. This new classroom can be a forest or a stream, an office or a lab, a museum or a zoo—anywhere real issues can be studied. Increasingly, the Digital Age is bringing these environments to students virtually, so that students in class or at home can travel via the Internet to a scientist's laboratory or a curator's collection.

Through project-based learning, students see that their learning has a purpose and is used every day in many fields of human endeavor. In person and through the Internet, they learn from many professionals, from engineers and artists to lawyers and architects, who are passionate about what they do and model positive habits of mind and work.

Just as project-based learning transforms curriculum, it shifts the assessment paradigm away from a focus on superficial assessment of rote learning. Through alternative methods, such as student portfolios, oral presentations, multimedia presentations, and review by experts and peers, assessment of project-based learning provides a more complete picture of student achievement, helping teachers and students to monitor and improve progress.

This book, *Increasing Student Learning Through Multimedia Projects*, covers all of these issues and more. It fulfills one of the great unmet needs in education—specific "field guides" to school reform. Much discussion of school reform adopts the view from 30,000 feet up, where lofty, high-sounding philosophy can be of little practical value unless grounded in real classrooms and the lives of real teachers and students. As the George Lucas Educational Foundation tells the success stories of technology in schools through film segments and Web content, people often respond by saying: "That's an inspiring story. How can I get started? What should I do Monday morning?"

This book answers those questions. It provides the philosophical rationale for project-based learning and supports it with the "ground truth" from teachers who have made project-based learning come alive in their classrooms.

Consider the challenge of making World War II history relevant to students born generations later. Fern Tavalin did so for her students by having them interview older relatives and friends; collect artifacts, such as the handkerchief given by a wife to a husband as he went off to war; and sing songs with a veteran.

The book's accounts of how project-based learning can be effective with all students are especially important. Students are encouraged to express their learning in forms that are most revealing of and true to their strengths and interests. At the same time, students working on projects must take greater responsibility for their own learning, even, at times, tutoring each other. Some schools are capitalizing on students' fluency with multimedia and making them technology teaching assistants, a new and powerful type of teacher-student relationship. Students as productive team members, insightful peer tutors, supportive teaching assistants, and even creative curriculum designers—these are the new roles our students will play in this Digital Age.

As students work in project teams, communicating with each other and managing relationships, they also are developing their social and emotional skills. Project-based learning enables classrooms to emphasize this undervalued part of the "invisible curriculum," what author Daniel Goleman has called "emotional intelligence." These skills prepare students well for working in the team-based workplace and also hold a little-known key to increasing student achievement: emotionally intelligent students often perform better on tests and other measures of learning because they are more equipped to concentrate, persist, and think independently.

The book also tells the story of the transformation of the teachers' own roles. These teachers have become conductors of a symphony of learning resources and experiences for their students. They refer to their new roles as project manager, facilitator, traffic cop, partner, consultant. They also relate how project-based learning has brought them closer through team teaching. The benefits of project-based collaboration are not just for students.

These teachers all agree on one thing: Project-based learning is a more exciting, challenging, and rewarding way to teach.

I have personally met some of the dedicated teachers whose work is reflected here and have seen some of their students' impressive multimedia products. I also am familiar with the research on the effectiveness of the Challenge 2000 Multimedia Project, which received original funding from the U.S. Department of Education and received recognition in 2000 as an exemplary educational technology project, one of only two in the United States.

There's a lot of wisdom in these pages to assist educators with both "the big picture" and "the small steps" needed to implement project-based learning. In giving teachers the step-by-step knowledge they need to implement project-based learning, this book is an owner's manual for a 21st century classroom.

MILTON CHEN
EXECUTIVE DIRECTOR
THE GEORGE LUCAS EDUCATIONAL FOUNDATION

Acknowledgments

We want to thank two groups of people, without whom this book would not have been possible. First, we thank the many (more than 140) teachers and Technology Learning Coordinators who participated in the Challenge 2000 Multimedia Project. In particular, we want to thank those whose words of wisdom, experience, and encouragement appear in the pages that follow:

Jean Babb

Clarence Bakken

Kay Banchero

Mary Fran Breiling

Dee Dee Bridges

Gayle Britt

Doug Day

Pam Ensign

Darrell Hendricks

Otak Jump

Charles Merritt

Ben Murray

Steve Pomeroy

Barbara Rawson

Linda Rusten

Penelope Sanders-Jones

Laura Silberstein

Jim Smith

Lucinda Surber

Linda Ullah

Ron Williamson

Nora Wolfe

Jeanine Woodell

Second, we are grateful to our many colleagues and supporters. Especially, we want to thank Joe Becerra, Olivia Clarke, Tim Cuneo, Shari Golan, Floyd Gonella, Peter Henschel, Ted Kahn, Jenelle Leonard, Ralph Manak, Jason

Marsh, Becky Morgan, Bill Penuel, Judy Powers, Ram Singh, and the staff of San Mateo County Office of Education. Finally, we want to express our gratitude to our editors at ASCD for their encouragement, patience, and wise counsel.

Introduction

In 1995, the Silicon Valley Challenge 2000 Multimedia Project—or the Multimedia Project, for short—was launched as one of the original 19 Technology Innovation Challenge Grants funded by the U.S. Department of Education. The purpose of these grants was to demonstrate, document, and disseminate cutting-edge ways technology could be used to improve education. The success of the Multimedia Project earned it recognition in September 2000 as one of only two educational technology programs nationwide to be cited as "exemplary" by the Department's Expert Panel on Educational Technology.

This book is based on the results of this award-winning program, and we hope it will provide you with an opportunity to share and build on our experience. We've written it with classroom teachers in mind, but we believe principals, staff developers, teacher educators, and anyone interested in the educational applications of technology will find it useful as well.

The goal of the Multimedia Project was to infuse the classrooms of Silicon Valley with an exemplary model of project-based multimedia learning. Accomplishing this goal required the combined efforts of many people playing complementary roles. One hundred and fifty classroom teachers (representing 50 schools in 11 school districts in the 1,740 square-mile Silicon Valley region) did the core work. For most of these teachers, multimedia was a new technology, and many had only passing experience with project-based learning. What they shared at the outset was an interest in learning more about technology and a desire to provide the best education possible for their students. As members of what came to be called the Project cadre, these teachers attended summer institutes and monthly workdays. They participated in online discussions. They used and contributed to the Project's Web site. They developed new relationships with colleagues from other schools and districts with whom they formed a strong community of practice. Through trial and error, exasperation, elation, and reflection, they shaped our concept of exemplary project-based multimedia learning and what it takes to make it happen in the classroom. You'll find the words and wisdom of these pioneer teachers highlighted throughout this book.

Supporting the cadre teachers was a special set of individuals who served in the role of Technology Learning Coordinator (TLC). These were experienced classroom teachers who were "early adopters" of technology and had become skilled technology users. Each TLC had responsibility for a team of four to six cadre members. Grant funds were used to release TLCs from some of their classroom teaching responsibilities, which enabled them to provide their cadre members with on-site coaching and support, to organize and lead local workshops, and to coordinate their team's participation in annual exhibitions of student work and other projectwide activities. The TLCs were a critical ingredient in the success of the Multimedia Project, and you'll find their words, too, featured many times in this book.

Several organizations made significant contributions to the Project. Researchers and theorists from the Institute for Research on Learning (IRL) and SRI International, both in Menlo Park, California, helped develop the Project's initial plan and provided a range of consultative services throughout its course. Joint Venture: Silicon Valley Network, a nonprofit regional organization composed of leaders from business, education, and government, provided an institutional "umbrella" that facilitated the necessary collaboration among schools and districts in the many different cities and communities of Silicon Valley. San Mateo and Santa Clara County Offices of Education helped in many ways such as providing fiscal oversight and meeting facilities and helping to integrate Project activities with other professional development programs already under way.

Each of the authors contributed in different ways to the Multimedia Project, as well as to this book. Barbara Means helped conceive the Project and, as director of the evaluation component, guided the design and execution of the research that documented the Project's progress and results. Karen Cole coordinated IRL's work on the Project with particular focus on supporting the TLCs in their mentoring role. In a sort of "sister project" exchange, Fern Tavalin, director of Vermont's WEB Project, came to Silicon Valley where she visited Project classrooms and "cross pollinated" the Multimedia Project with the experiences of the WEB Project. Michael Simkins directed the Project.

This book is part of a set of complementary resources on project-based multimedia learning that includes a CD-ROM, a video, and a Web site. In the book, we have sought to balance theory and practice as well as formality and informality. By combining the perspectives of researchers, project staff, and classroom teachers experienced in project-based multimedia learning, we hope to provide you with conceptually sound and thoroughly practical advice. Although we certainly do not claim that this is the only way to teach, or even the only way to approach the integration of multimedia technology in the classroom, we do know that it is an effective model with proven results. We hope you'll find this to be a useful and "user-friendly" guidebook. We also invite you to become part of our community by sharing your projects, your reflections, and *yourself* at our Web site (http://pblmm.k12.ca.us). Join us. We look forward to seeing you there.

1

What Is Project-Based Multimedia Learning?

Entering Mrs. Baxter's classroom, you first notice that every child is completely engrossed. Second, you notice the cacophony of voices, rising and falling in intense, animated discussions among small groups of 3rd graders.

You look for the teacher—she isn't conveniently located at the front of the room. Finally, you see her down among a group of students. You wait for her to notice you as she shows the group how to use the index of a book to find information about shelter for a tribe of Native Americans.

As you wait, your eyes move from group to group. At the computers, three boys are typing some text they have composed for their presentations. A group of girls paints a colorful scene of a Native American village to be scanned into the presentation software later. Another group of boys uses a Venn diagram to show foods in their own diet, foods in "their" tribe's diet, and foods they have in common. You want to ask them about their work but can't bear to break their concentration.

Mrs. Baxter notices you and starts toward you, but each group of students she passes stops her to proudly show off their work or ask her to check something. She finally reaches you and starts to explain the various activities the children are working on to prepare their multimedia presentations—content research, art, language arts, math, and technology activities she has designed for the project. You talk for almost 10 minutes before you notice the most amazing thing of all—*the children are all still working*, still engrossed, still animated and focused.

●   ●   ●

Project-based learning is an old and respected educational method. The use of multimedia is a dynamic new form of communication. The merging of project-based learning and multimedia represents a powerful teaching strategy that we call "project-based multimedia learning." This book provides background information and guidelines for developing and implementing your own units based on this strategy.

Defining Project-Based Multimedia Learning

It's best to start with some definitions. By project-based learning, we mean a teaching method in which students acquire new knowledge and skills in the course of designing, planning, and producing some product or performance. By multimedia, we mean the integration of media objects such as text, graphics, video, animation, and sound to represent and convey information. Thus, our definition is:

> Project-based multimedia learning is a method of teaching in which
> students acquire new knowledge and skills in the course of designing,
> planning, and producing a *multimedia product.*

Your students' multimedia products will be technology-based presentations, such as a computerized slide show, a Web site, or a video. These presentations will include evidence that your students have mastered key concepts and processes you need to teach and will be a source of great pride for them and for you.

Dimensions of Project-Based Multimedia Learning

Project-based multimedia learning has seven key dimensions: core curriculum, real-world connection, extended time frame, student decision making, collaboration, assessment, and multimedia. Like air, fire, water, and earth, it's possible to have one of these dimensions present without the rest. A strong unit, however, includes them all. Here is a brief explanation of each.

Core curriculum. At the foundation of any unit of this type is a clear set of learning goals drawn from whatever curriculum or set of standards is in use. We use the term *core* to emphasize that project-based multimedia learning should address the basic knowledge and skills all students are expected to acquire, and should not simply be an enrichment or extra-credit activity for a special few. Often, these projects lend themselves well to multidisciplinary or cross-curricular approaches.

Real-world connection. Like the Velveteen Rabbit in Margery Williams's famous story, project-based multimedia learning strives to be real. It seeks to connect students' work in school with the wider world in which students live.

"Real life!" Now, that is the key!
I spent years waiting for "real life"
to begin, not realizing that my child-
hood was real life. Children, even
young ones, can make a meaningful
contribution to the world while they
are learning.
　　　　　—TECHNOLOGY LEARNING
　　　　　　　　　　COORDINATOR

You may design this feature into a project by means of the content chosen,
the types of activities, the types of products, or in other ways. What is critical
is that the students—not only the teacher—perceive what is *real* about the
project.

Extended time frame. A good project is not a one-shot lesson; it extends
over a significant period of time. The actual length of a project may vary with
the age of the students and the nature of the project. It may be days, weeks,
or months. What's important is that students experience a succession of challenges that culminates in a substantial final product from which they can
derive pride and a clear sense of accomplishment.

Student decision making. In project-based multimedia learning, students have a say. Teachers look carefully at what decisions have to be made
and divide them into "teacher's" and "students'" based on a clear rationale.
For example, a teacher might limit students to a single authoring program to
minimize complications that might arise were students allowed to use any
software they chose. And yet she can also give students considerable leeway
in determining what substantive content would be included in their projects.
Though the teacher is clearly in charge, she tries to enlarge the area for students to make decisions about the form and content of their final products,
as well as the process for producing them.

Collaboration. We define collaboration *as working together jointly to
accomplish a common intellectual purpose in a manner superior to what
might have been accomplished working alone.* Students may work in pairs
or in teams of as many as five or six. Whole-class collaborations are also possible. The goal is for each student involved to make a separate contribution to
the final work and for the whole to be greater than the sum of the parts.
Collaborative projects not only involve many features of typical cooperative

learning strategies but also transcend them in this focus on synergy and the production of a jointly authored multimedia product.

Assessment. Regardless of the teaching method used, data must be gathered on what students have learned. When using project-based multimedia learning, teachers face additional assessment challenges because multimedia products by themselves do not represent a full picture of student learning. Students are gaining content information, becoming better team members, solving problems, and making choices about what new information to show in their presentations. We consider assessment to have three different roles in the project-based multimedia context:

- Activities for developing expectations;
- Activities for improving the media products; and
- Activities for compiling and disseminating evidence of learning.

Multimedia. In multimedia projects, students do not learn simply by "using" multimedia produced by others; they learn by creating it themselves. The development of such programs as HyperStudio, Kid Pix, and Netscape Composer has made it possible for students of all ages to become the authors of multimedia content. As students design and research their projects, instead of gathering only written notes, they also gather—and create—pictures, video clips, recordings, and other media objects that will later serve as the raw material for their final product.

I did a project a couple of years ago where students drew on index cards that were later filmed. Although the students were still excited to be creating animation, those who were not as good at art started losing interest toward the end. With the use of computers, even an animated stick figure looks pretty good, and students are given the opportunity of cutting and pasting. The use of computers lowers many of the barriers that limited some students' ability to creatively express themselves . . . Boys, girls, high achievers, and low achievers seemed equally motivated to create a quality product.

—MIDDLE SCHOOL TEACHER

An Example

A teacher we know teaches 7th graders social studies. Her students, as part of their studies of medieval history, created a multimedia presentation about the Black Plague. She teamed with a teacher in the science department for the unit. In science, students created animations that simulated how the plague virus attacks the body. In social studies, they created computer-based presentations looking at the plague from various perspectives that included 14th century farmers and 21st century scientists. Their presentations used primary historical sources, as well as literature and current events. The presentation compared the plague to the AIDS epidemic of today.

The Black Plague project was exemplary in terms of the seven dimensions mentioned earlier. It addressed state and district standards in social studies, science, and technology. The real-world connection to the AIDS epidemic made the project relevant for students. The project extended over many weeks, and students were allowed to choose perspectives and make decisions about the design and interface for their presentations. Students collaborated in small groups to research and implement each perspective in the presentation. Assessment was ongoing and multifaceted. Students' presentations included a variety of media: text, original artwork, scanned images, and animations.

Why Use Project-Based Multimedia Learning?

Teaching methods abound—some sound, some not so sound. If you have been teaching for many years, you've no doubt seen several new ways of teaching come into vogue. Some have taken hold; many have faded away; a few have become infamous. In their book *Models of Teaching*, Bruce Joyce and Marsha Weil with Emily Calhoun (2000) describe no fewer than 20 ways to teach. Like different health remedies, all these teaching methods clamor for your attention, and each urges you to include it in your teacher's medicine cabinet. With so many options, why should you choose project-based multimedia learning?

The answer lies in the concept of "value added." Project-based multimedia learning can add value to your teaching. In economics, value is added to a product when it is somehow made better or more useful to the consumer. Although we don't use the term much in everyday life, we are surrounded by examples. Our cereal has vitamins that are not part of the basic grains. The bottle of "one step" shampoo in the shower includes a conditioner. On vacation, we stay at a motel that offers complimentary drinks at happy hour and a free breakfast in the morning. You already have strategies for teaching your curriculum, so what "value" do you add when you implement project-based multimedia learning? In their book, *Teaching the New Basic Skills*, Richard Murnane and Frank Levy (1996) describe three skill sets students need to be competitive for today's jobs:

- Hard skills (math, reading, and problem-solving skills mastered at a much higher level than previously expected of high school graduates);
- Soft skills (for example, the ability to work in a group and to make effective oral and written presentations); and
- The ability to use a personal computer to carry out routine tasks (for example, word processing, data management, and creating multimedia presentations).

In its 1991 report, the Secretary of Labor's Commission on Achieving Necessary Skills (popularly known as "SCANS") noted that to find meaningful work, high school graduates need to master a combination of *foundation skills* and *competencies*. Besides typical basic skills, foundation skills include thinking skills, such as reasoning, making decisions, thinking creatively, and solving problems, as well as personal qualities such as responsibility and self-management. Required competencies include:

- Identifying, organizing, planning, and allocating time, money, materials, and workers.
- Negotiating, exercising leadership, working with diversity, teaching others new skills, serving clients and customers, and participating as a team member.
- Selecting technology, applying technology to a task, and maintaining and troubleshooting technology.

These are exactly the sorts of skills students learn when engaged in project-based multimedia learning.

Teachers who have implemented project-based multimedia learning over time cite other benefits. It is a powerful motivator and engages students who might otherwise tune out. Students engaged in the creation of multimedia projects spend more time on task, even to the point of devoting recess, lunch, and after-school time to the work. The work they do tends to be more complex. Sharing their final products with peers, parents, and others affords students an intense sense of pride and accomplishment that rarely accompanies the completion of a term paper or set of textbook exercises.

I try to have the students think of the project as a real job. They fill out job applications, undergo interviews, and have real products to be completed within a time structure.

—TECHNOLOGY LEARNING COORDINATOR

Adding Project-Based Multimedia Learning to Your Teaching Repertoire

Being a teacher is a bit like being a personal trainer. In general, a trainer knows that all clients need a balanced workout. They need to develop muscular strength, flexibility, and aerobic fitness. They also need to adhere to a sound, balanced diet. At the same time, each client will have specific needs or conditions that require accommodation. The workout you design for your client with asthma will be different from the one you create for your client with arthritis.

Likewise, effective teachers employ various teaching methods to achieve a balanced instructional program that is also personalized and reflects the needs and interests of individual students. You know that your students need a balanced diet of academic content and process skills—and workouts that include learning, practicing, analyzing, reflecting, and assessing. You also know that students vary in their comfort with these activities and the amount of support they need.

Project-based multimedia learning is one instructional strategy that you can use in a school year that may also include non-technical projects, lecture and note-taking, rote practice, writing, and artistic or creative work. During this part of the year, students may be spending less time on rote practice and the breadth of material they cover may be smaller. What they will be doing instead includes:

- Honing their planning and organizational skills;
- Learning to present information in compelling ways;
- Synthesizing and analyzing complex content and data;

The amazing transformation I witnessed in my students came with the publishing of the first student work on the Web. The transformation had to do with the concept of audience. Realizing that their work was posted for the world to see, the students suddenly became more careful about their research, documentation, and the mechanics of their writing. The most reluctant proofreaders became voracious proofreaders and insistent editors. I no longer had to correct their work—they took an active interest in making sure that what was published was accurate and well written.

—TECHNOLOGY LEARNING COORDINATOR

We worked on the project on and off for much of the year. At the beginning, I would let the students work on the project one day every week or so. When that day came, students would pump their arms and say, "Yes!" The students were so into the project that the class just basically ran itself. I would wander the room getting group updates and be available to help with individual group problems. Students were always asking for more time on the computers, even 10 minutes here and there. Sometimes students would hang around for hours after school; when their parents came to pick them up they would have a hard time getting the students to leave.

—MIDDLE SCHOOL TEACHER

- Practicing research and technical skills; and
- Learning how academic subject matter applies to the real world.

Further, the motivational character keeps students engaged, giving you the freedom to support individual students—far better than when every moment of instruction depends on you alone.

Considering giving project-based multimedia learning a try? The next chapters provide specific strategies—all classroom tested—for making your project a success. We have consolidated the experience of scores of teachers and teacher leaders who have used project-based multimedia learning. They have contributed their stories and suggestions so that you can avoid the pitfalls they experienced and more quickly enjoy the rewards.

2
A Multimedia Primer

This chapter might have been titled, "What You Always Wanted to Know About Multimedia but Were Afraid to Ask." We've found that when we talk about technology, it's generally better to err on the side of explaining too much, not too little. If you're already an experienced multimedia author and producer, feel free to skip this chapter. It's intended to provide teachers new to multimedia with enough information to have a successful first experience with project-based multimedia learning.

What does the term *multimedia* really mean? Though actually plural in its spelling, multimedia represents a "singular" integration of media objects, such as text, graphics, video, animation, and sound, to represent and convey information. (Don't be put off by the term "objects." Substitute "elements" or "ingredients" or simply "stuff.") Although not all types of media objects must be included in a given presentation, multimedia gets its name because at least several such media elements are combined in one communication.

Multimedia Is a Communication Tool

Imagine that you've shared your painstakingly planned unit with your students and they are excited about the prospect of creating a multimedia presentation. What exactly will they be doing? They'll be figuring out what they want to communicate and, using a computer, combining different types of media to create a presentation customized to their intended audience. Along the way, they'll need to choose pictures, text, video, sounds, and animation, and bring all these pieces together in such a way that their message gets across in an efficient and compelling manner. That is the art of making multimedia.

Audience is a key word. The point of making a multimedia presentation is to communicate a message to an audience. Keeping this purpose in mind will help you and your students remain focused on communication rather than getting sidetracked by the complexities of computer technology. A good multimedia production blends both aesthetic and technical considerations to achieve an overall effect. This chapter will present the basics of both to get you off to a successful start.

Though the purpose of multimedia is communication, the purpose of a project of this type is to provide a rich learning opportunity for students. That being the case, you must consider what kinds of media make practical sense to include, taking into account your expertise and that of your students in dealing with various elements. How much students learn counts more than a fancy product. The trick is to design your project so that technical difficulties do not eclipse your learning goals, while allowing your students the capability to make compelling presentations.

How do you make multimedia? In general, you construct your media pieces separately in programs dedicated to making a particular type of media, and then you use a program called an "authoring tool" to combine the different types of media into a single presentation. For example, you edit images in an image editor and construct animation sequences in an animation program. Then you put the finished images and animations together with an authoring tool. The authoring tool allows you to design and format your presentation with, perhaps, an image at the top, some text underneath, and a "start" button on the right to begin the animation.

Five Basic Types of Media Objects

There are really only five basic types of media objects you will generally use, and no one says you have to use all five, especially your first time out. We will discuss all five in this chapter—why you choose them, how you make them, and how you might overcome difficulties associated with them. Remember, you don't have to be an expert with any of these—even knowing the technical and artistic basics will allow your students to construct effective and engaging presentations. So here we go. The five types are:

1. Images. Images come in many forms. A few notable types include graphs, maps, photographs, and drawings.

2. Text. This includes everything from image captions to paragraphs of information.

3. Sound. A few examples are voice recordings, music, and sound effects. Sounds can be used alone or to enhance another media element.

4. *Motion.* This includes cartoon-type animation, video, and moving transitions between screens of media.

5. *Interactivity.* This means making buttons, hyperlinks, and the like. Your students, as designers of the presentation, can select an assortment of experiences so users can tailor a multimedia tour to their own needs and interests.

One more thing—this chapter does contain some detailed technical information about some of the media types. If you start to feel you're getting in over your head, skim sections now to get the general idea, and then come back to them later when you know what media you will be using in your own project.

Images

Two questions to consider about images are "Is the content engaging?" and "Is the technical quality high enough for the audience to interpret it?" Addressing these basic questions will dramatically improve your ability to communicate using visual images.

As you and your students select or create images for your multimedia production, take some time to look at pictures that you consider appealing. Because the subject matter is compelling, you become involved. The technical quality is probably high, too. Think about composition. Images that place the subject matter dead center are static, so place the main subject a little off-center (see Figures 2.1 and 2.2).

Taking photographs, scanning, downloading noncopyrighted pictures, and creating in a drawing program are the four most common ways of making images for computer use.

FIGURE 2.1

The "Lower First Molar" chart on the blackboard adds an element of surprise to this photo of what might have otherwise been a "high military strategy" session.

FIGURE 2.2

The angle of the camera and the open mouths create an unusual image that moves the eye from one point to another.

These two photos are part of a series that students assembled and scanned from family photo albums to represent interesting images.

Taking photographs. Viewers' eyes will be drawn away from images that are out of focus, overexposed, or poor in contrast. Most still cameras in classrooms today set focus and exposure automatically, but many allow you to make decisions about the flash and have special settings for bright daylight and low light conditions. Video cameras usually allow you to choose either manual or autofocus. You can check the camera manuals if you want to help your students use these features—it's easier to work with an image that starts out good than to try to improve its quality later with software. You can also set

Imaging software can really do a lot to make an image more powerful. The software lets you "crop" or cut out parts of a photo that don't relate to your message. With cropping, you can take an image at the side of the photo and make it the center, or take an image at the center and move it off-center to make the photo less static. The imaging software also lets you improve the contrast of a picture or brighten it.

up the cameras in advance if you know the conditions under which students will be taking photographs.

You do not need digital cameras to create multimedia—you can use a regular camera, develop the pictures, and scan them (see the next section). Digital cameras are easier to work with because all media must ultimately be converted to digital format. They simply allow you to skip the conversion step. They also let you see your photograph right away, so you know immediately if you have what you need. Finally, making an initial investment in a digital camera means you no longer have to pay for film or developing services.

Scanning. Scanning is probably the most common way that students create images for multimedia projects. Students can place any paper image on a scanning machine, or "scanner," and the image appears on the computer screen. They then save the image and edit it with imaging software. Students typically scan original artwork or, with permission, photographs from books. Having them create original artwork for scanning, where appropriate for the topic, has many advantages. For example, it gives students "offline" tasks to do while other students use the computers. You avoid all copyright and fair-use issues. And students love seeing their artwork on the screen—it looks bright, shiny, and professional.

Downloading noncopyrighted images. Using images from the Internet is increasingly common because it is so easy to do. Students can save images with their browser and import them directly into their own presentations. Copyright issues are important here—material on most Web sites is not in the public domain. It is easy to send an e-mail request for educational permission to use privately held images, text, sounds, and other materials. Multimedia projects are an excellent occasion for teaching your students about such concepts as intellectual property, copyright, and fair use. One good resource is the Copyright and Fair Use site at Stanford University, http://fairuse .Stanford.edu.

Creating images in a drawing program. Finally, students can create images with a drawing or painting program like Kid Pix, Painter, or Illustrator. These images can be saved and imported into presentations.

Although each of these ways of creating comes with separate procedures depending on what software is used, there are certain common aspects. Most notably, images for multimedia are designed for viewing on a video or computer monitor, rather than on paper. This makes your job easier because, although printing has a whole set of difficult rules and formulas, preparing images for the screen requires only a few simple guidelines:

- Make sure that your image resolution is set to 72 dpi ("dots per inch") so that the viewable size stays the way you want it. Your image-editing software allows you to do this easily.
- Test the color of your images on several different computer screens so that you are not surprised by how much your colors vary from screen to screen.
- Use a Web-based color scale if you are preparing images for the World Wide Web. Most software allows you to choose "Only Web Colors" in the color selector. If you have this option, use it.

Text

Text has been one of the most baffling elements to handle in the move to multimedia forms of expression. The first educational uses of multimedia relied heavily on traditional notions—the more information, the better.

Thus, in the early days of multimedia production, many students re-created picture encyclopedias with detailed written descriptions and some accompanying images. Unfortunately, lots of text, especially in small font sizes, does not translate well to many multimedia products. So knowing how much text to use for which purpose you have in mind is key.

The three separate functions for text include information communication, enhancement of other media, and artistic expression.

Information Communication. The Web allows anyone, anywhere the opportunity to publish information. Web sites use the largest amount of text of all multimedia forms of presentation. Web users are familiar with large amounts of text on the screen because they are usually searching for information. If you are planning a presentation that is information-rich and requires text to communicate the message, think about building a Web site.

Enhancement of Other Media. Rather than being the primary vehicle for carrying information, text in a stand-alone presentation becomes a more equal partner with other media. That means that the use of text has to stay in balance with the use of the other elements. Most people watch, rather than print from, computer-based presentations. Therefore, you need to give extra consideration to the amount of text you use, the size of the font, and the type of the font. A general rule is, the fewer words, the better. This means carefully selecting text that is then used sparingly.

In a classroom setting, it is often helpful to ask students to prepare written statements of learning or to make an accompanying brochure so that they can demonstrate the content knowledge gained from the project-based multimedia experience. In that way, students do not have to overuse text in the presentation itself but can still express the fullness of their learning.

Artistic Expression. Students enjoy playing with words in unconventional ways. Many people design multimedia presentations that mix capital letters with lower case, or create shapes with words, and so forth. Phrases or flying text that defy most of the conventions we teach in a language arts class become energizing aspects of a multimedia presentation. In this sense, the use of text becomes more like the use of an image and takes on artistic characteristics (see Figure 2.3).

Text is easy; you can construct it in almost every authoring program. That's probably why most people overuse it. Keep these things in mind when creating your text:

- Select colors that coordinate well and enhance the message you are trying to send.
- Keep text to a minimum. It's a good editing exercise for students to find the essential words that convey a message.

Talk to an art teacher or an artist about complementary colors and font types. Two excellent books that can help you are *The Non-Designer's Web Book* by Robin Williams and John Tollett (2000) and *Web Style Guide: Basic Design Principles for Creating Web Sites* by Patrick Lynch and Sarah Horton (1999).

Sound

Sound is the most frequently overlooked ingredient in presentations. But the quality of the audio track can either make or break the show. A few well-chosen and well-spoken words can take the place of pages of text on a

FIGURE 2.3

In this multimedia retelling of "Why Mosquitoes Buzz in People's Ears," students chose to use the word "buzz" to show annoyance.
—Walden School, Walden, VT

screen; music inserted at just the right moment can evoke any emotion; exciting sounds can enhance a story or visual presentation.

Fortunately, getting high-quality sound on most new computers is fairly simple. It usually means connecting a microphone, tape recorder, or video camera to the "sound in" connection on your computer, calling up some simple software, and clicking the "record" button. For simple voice recordings and the like, you can use the sound recorders that come with most computers. Check your equipment—if there is a microphone with your computer hardware, then your system probably has a sound recorder. For more complex audio needs, programs such as Final Cut Pro allow for more precise editing, special effects, and processing to improve the sound quality.

Be sure to monitor the sound (listen through headphones) as you record or immediately afterward to make sure you are getting what you want and that the sound levels are not too high. Every time the levels go above a certain range (usually shown in red on sound meters), "clipping" occurs. This makes your sounds scratchy or distorted.

Unlike a tape recorder that records sounds continuously, a computer "samples" sound—that is, it "listens" intermittently and records what it hears at set intervals. The interval length determines the quality of the sound when it's replayed. Shorter intervals make for higher quality sound, but they also take up more memory. For the most part, the finished sound to be played in your presentations can be 8 bits, sampled at 22 kilohertz (kHz). You will find these numbers in the "settings" of your recording software.

Although higher settings give better sound, they also take up more room in your computer's memory. Not having enough memory to run large files leads to playback problems. Keep this in mind if your presentation is to be played on other computers with less memory. Having students test different sampling rates to judge the trade-off between sound quality and file size is a great math exercise.

Using Voice. Like everything else, voice in a multimedia presentation should be used in balanced amounts. Generally, audiences enjoy the authenticity of voice, but hearing is not the most efficient way for them to get large amounts of information—it takes too long to listen. Keep the communicative purpose of multimedia in mind, and use voice where inflections and emotion communicate what text could not.

Two major impediments to getting high-quality voice recordings are insufficient volume (either the speaker is too soft or the microphone is too far away) and enunciation. If your students are audiotaping themselves, don't miss the chance to teach the fundamentals of oral expression, articulation, and public speaking.

Using Music. Many schools have music-composition programs. This is the richest source of music for presentations. Students can compose pieces that are specifically designed to accompany your multimedia products. Singing songs or recording student improvisations made from simple instruments found in your music classrooms are lively ways to incorporate music, as well. If you must use "canned music," make sure that you have copyright permission.

Using Sounds. A few well-placed sounds (or noise) can create an audio impression. Indeed, early radio production developed the use of sound effects into an art form. Many authoring programs come with built-in sounds, but it's much more fun to create your own. If your students use sound, especially to move from one scene to another (called a transition), make sure that their sounds enhance the movement. Many beginning multimedia projects

A group of 7th graders put together a multimedia presentation about their grandparents. One of the students had just learned how to make audio files and decided to create voice-only links to information. During the in-progress design review, the group quickly identified instances when voice did or didn't help. For example, they did not enjoy listening to long stories without accompanying images or motion.

An elder interviewee and a student worked together on a presentation on World War II memories and produced an extremely poignant recording of a song from the era. As the recording played, the presentation displayed collages of photographs and other memorabilia.

rely on built-in sounds such as "jaws" or "machine guns" that are randomly placed and distracting.

Motion

Screen transitions, video clips, and animations are the major types of motion in multimedia productions. Because the concept of screen motion shares a lot with physical dance, it is helpful to think in terms of the use of space, time, and energy. A dancer moves across the stage by jumping high or falling low, sometimes slowly and sometimes quickly, interacting with music to create the energy that becomes the complete visual and emotional display that we call dance. Your computer screen is much like a dance stage. Motion elements enter from one side of the stage, move about the stage for a certain time, getting larger or smaller, moving slowly or quickly to create an impression or send a message. Where your animation travels on the screen depends on how you use the space. How long it takes is determined by your use of time. A sense of energy is created by the size (and change of size) of animated objects, combined with the speed (and change of speed) with which they travel.

Screen Transitions. Keeping in mind the metaphor of dance, remember that screen transitions allow you to add a sense of rhythm and timing to your presentation. A transition acts as a visually interesting pause between screens of content. Transitions can convey meaning, such as signaling a topic shift or a shift in the level of detail.

Screen transitions are built into most multimedia authoring systems and help the user navigate from one page to another. The simplest transitions are called "fades" or "dissolves," in which the old screen fades away and the new one comes slowly into view. Another common transition is a "wipe," where the old screen appears to slide off one side of the screen and the new one slides on. Software for stand-alone presentations contains many built-in options for creating transitions. Programs such as Macromedia's Flash permit a type of transition on the Web as objects appear and disappear.

Fades are the least obtrusive transition. Applying a fade to each transition as an initial step can help you estimate the overall timing of your presentation. Then, you can carefully select other transitions to enhance the presentation.

Think about the purpose of each transition. Does it represent an idea? Does it create an energy or feeling that enhances the idea it represents? Are the transitions overly repetitive? Do they change too frequently for no apparent reason? Sometimes transitions add glitz to a presentation, but they are frequently overused or misused (see Figure 2.4).

Video Clips. Video clips play a special role in multimedia production. Unlike full-screen video, where the video tells an entire story, clips are used in multimedia to convey pieces of information or ideas. In one project on Newton's laws of motion, students mixed text and diagrams about science content with video clips to demonstrate concepts like inertia.

Four steps to creating good clips include shooting footage, logging tape contents, digitizing segments into your computer, and preparing files for use in your presentation. Each of these stages takes a certain amount of preparation and forethought before starting.

1. Shooting footage. Always consider who or what you are going to shoot and why you are using video as an element in your presentation when planning a videotaping session. Check your video camera manual for camera

FIGURE 2.4

Students selected a transition named "Zoom Open" to make this owl seem to appear from nowhere as he entered the multimedia stage. The transition was coupled with a reverberating sound to establish the owl as a powerful and wise character.
—Walden School, Walden, VT

First-time media producers enjoy using transitions such as one called "jaws," which appears to "chew" the image until it disappears. This type of transition might work well in a presentation for dramatic effect, but it interferes when applied between images that give somber messages or relate basic information.

techniques to share with your students. Beyond camera technique, keep a few other things in mind for best results:

• Remind students to make sure the camera is steady (and placed on a tripod when possible), the connectors are clean and securely fastened, and the image is well lit and in focus.

• Movement (changes from frame to frame) creates larger file sizes. So avoid active-motion backgrounds and camera panning (moving the camera from side to side) unless it's absolutely necessary.

• Encourage students to use close-up shots whenever possible. These are easier to see on a computer screen.

• When using a tripod, secure the area so no one trips on a cable or knocks over the camera. Carry duct tape in your camera bag, and use it to fasten the cables to the floor.

• Most cameras have a setting that allows you to imprint a time and date stamp directly onto your video image. Make sure this option is off unless you want it in the finished product—it's nearly impossible to delete the time stamp once it's on your image.

2. Logging tape contents. When lots of students are shooting video, it is easy to lose track of what each tape contains. Before taping, make sure that the videotape and its storage box are clearly marked with the name of the contents. After shooting, ask students to make a log or inventory of where important information resides on the tape. This log can be a simple list of major events or, if students need extra practice with language arts, it can become a more elaborate list of transcribed quotations from interviewees.

Some things to keep in mind include:

• Most cameras have a time display that you can turn on as you log. Writing down the time code numbers for major events helps you keep track of where important information resides. On some cameras, this is the same function that puts a time stamp on the tape during recording, so remind students to turn it off before shooting the next sequence.

• If students log tape using a machine other than the camera that recorded the tape, they should note what machine they used to create each log. Unless you are using digital video, times can vary greatly from machine to machine.

• The log is for the functional purpose of locating information to select what to use and what to discard. Try not to make the process overly tedious by requiring detailed logs that do not serve this purpose.

Remember, creating the log is an important step in the discipline of shooting and editing video. Don't leave it out!

3. Digitizing segments. Once you have shot your footage, you must bring it into your computer to prepare it for presentation. This is called "digitizing." Computers that digitize video have cables that run from your camera to your computer. The cables access a software program that converts the camera information into computer information. If the video footage you'd like to include in your presentation is not continuous (meaning you'd like a piece from here and another piece from there), you'll need a special program to edit clips. Previously, teachers might copy portions of video from one VCR to another. Luckily, popular computer programs like Avid Cinema, Final Cut Pro, and Apple's i-Movie and QuickTime Pro do that job much more easily now.

One professional producer makes it a practice to avoid pausing the tape while logging. That way logging never takes longer than watching the tape, and the level of detail is automatically kept appropriately low. Students may be able to do this if they work with a partner—one writes or types while the other watches and controls the playback.

The programs themselves have specific directions to follow. Beyond these directions, keep the following points in mind:

- For most purposes, bringing video into the computer at quarter-screen or half-screen size works better than full-screen size.
- Make sure that you have enough storage space on your computer to handle digitized video clips. They take up a lot of room.
- Compress your files to reduce size. Compression eliminates some of the video information so that the file size becomes smaller. Select a compression type from your video software. In many programs, a dialog box about size and compression appears on your screen before the software is fully loaded. Experiment with the different types of compression that your software offers to select the one that works best for you.

4. Preparing files for presentation. Digitized video is created in its native file format. You should convert it into a file type that can be read universally by any computer that handles video. For instance, if you use Avid Cinema to digitize video, the files are in the native language of Cinema. They should be converted into a QuickTime file or some other file type that will be read easily by computers that do not have Cinema installed. (See the section "Putting the Elements Together" for more information on file formats.) In simple programs, this is as easy as selecting the "Save As" command from the "Edit" menu. More complex programs, such as Media Cleaner Pro, have a menu of choices that help you carefully select how you want to compress and convert your files.

Whether you choose a simple "Save As" command in your video software, or export your file into something complex, do not overlook this important step. Forgetting to do this has disappointed many young users at presentation time when they must show their presentations on a different computer from the one that created them.

Animation. Two common types of animation are found in multimedia production: two-dimensional (2-D) cel and three-dimensional (3-D) rendering. Cel animation is based on drawing one image after another with slight changes in position to create a sense of movement. Early cartoons were drawn as cel animation. In addition to their drawing capabilities, some authoring programs include an animation feature that allows the user to move an object across the screen without changing it, thus creating a 2-D motion effect.

3-D rendering is currently popular with many students because newly developed software helps them to easily create a three-dimensional sense of space. Animation can be used for artistic expression, to model concepts in science and other subject areas, or to show all sides of a three-dimensional object such as a museum artifact.

Interactivity

Multimedia is an unusual form of communication because it allows users to shape their own paths through the media. One user can navigate through a presentation in a totally different way from the next just by clicking different links or making different choices from a menu. Designers must think through how different members of their audience may use their presentation, and they must organize media so all users can find what they are looking for.

Authoring programs allow you to add interactivity—you don't need a separate program. The simplest form of interactivity is the slide show in which a user decides when to advance each frame. From there, interactivity becomes more complex, reaching its height with sophisticated computer games. (Don't worry, you're not making those!) Most classroom projects have buttons, hyperlinks, and menu choices as their major forms of interactivity.

Balancing an easy-to-use navigational structure with a degree of user control is a challenge for multimedia design. Good organization and consistency in interface design help a user to maintain an orientation while navigating through simple or complex structures. If you have a lot of hyperlinks or buttons that lead to other parts of your presentation, the user can get lost and confused. The following are easy ways for students to establish a clear navigation path:

• Check the storyboard. If the lines connecting various screens resemble a plate of spaghetti, you have a problem. An easy structure to use is a hierarchy as illustrated in Figure 2.5.

• Make sure that the buttons are placed consistently and look the same from screen to screen.

• Use color or design to let the users know which section of the presentation they are in.

• Include a navigation bar on each page that allows the user to return to the home page or the main page of each section.

> **FIGURE 2.5 SAMPLE STORYBOARD**
>
>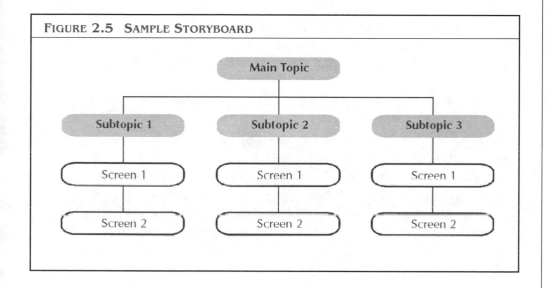

Putting the Elements Together

Assembling media elements into a whole is known as authoring. Multimedia authoring can take many forms, but for your purposes, you and your students will likely be creating Web pages or computer based media presentations. If you have Netscape Communicator on your computer, you already have a very simple Web authoring tool called Composer. Other Web authoring applications include Dreamweaver, HomeSite, GoLive, and FrontPage. Computer based media presentations are a modern version of a "slide show." Common tools for this type of authoring are PowerPoint and HyperStudio. More sophisticated tools include Director, Authorware, and eZedia.

Authoring software serves as an assembler for the media files that you have created in other programs. The part of authoring that may require the most technical knowledge is saving each media piece in a compatible file format.

Think of each piece of software as speaking its own language ("native" file format). When you use Photoshop, for instance, your file is created as a Photoshop file type. If you want another program to "understand" your Photoshop file, the other program must be able to translate Photoshop. If it can't, you need to convert your Photoshop file into a "universal" file format that the other software can speak. Some common universal file formats for images include jpgs, gifs, and picts. The authoring program you select will tell you which file types it can talk to. Refer to the manual to find out what file types you need to make so that your media files will be accepted by your authoring program. This process is not as difficult as it may seem. Changing the file type to a universal format is usually as easy as selecting the "Save As" option and choosing the correct file type from a pull-down menu.

Keeping It Simple

Breaking a large project into pieces makes it more manageable. Consider a project with six distinct segments: two art projects and four writing pieces. As you introduce each segment, discuss how much class time to reserve for the project. Younger (and less experienced) students often have few time management skills. For the first few segments, students may not have a realistic idea of how much time to allow. (Teachers attempting their first multimedia project will find they have the same tendency to underestimate the amount of time necessary to complete a project!) Frequent checks on progress and

My 4th grade class worked as a whole group to produce our Pixies & Paintings multimedia project. For each segment of the project, students worked in pairs to create a work of art or a piece of writing. The partner pieces formed individual pages of a class Web site.

—ELEMENTARY TEACHER

revision of the schedule help students begin to develop a more realistic understanding of the time required to complete a segment.

Planning a project with similar segments allows the teacher to guide more students through successive stages with increased individual responsibility. You can begin each segment by reviewing what went well and identifying trouble spots in previous segments. Encourage students to choose a specific skill to work on in each segment. Progress in meeting these goals can be the focus for class discussions.

Introducing the technical skills needed is easy to manage when students are working together. Try using a TV monitor connection to give a quick overview of a program or skill to the whole class and then teach pairs of students to be responsible for teaching subsequent pairs. Students love the chance to be the "experts." Be sure all have a chance to be expert at some point.

The whole-group model is a good entry point for multimedia projects for both students and teachers. It is easy for the teacher to manage and ensures success for all students. The end product is an impressive piece of work that students (and teachers!) are proud to share with others. After completing a group project, both students and teacher will have the confidence and skills necessary to complete individual multimedia projects.

You could spend a lifetime learning what there is to know about any one of the media elements. A teacher's job is not to be a professional media developer. To keep from becoming overwhelmed by all of the information and skills that are possible to acquire, limit what you want to learn before you begin your first venture. Then, acquire new skills slowly as the need for them arises. For example, one teacher did a slide show presentation with only text and images as a first step. In just two days, she learned how to prepare images for display and how to insert text. Her next step was to ask students to design slide shows. Then, she decided to learn how to take the slide shows and place them into a simple authoring program where users could select which shows they wanted to see and when they wanted to see them. With this simple baseline of knowledge, the teacher felt competent to manage a more complex project with her students.

To take things at a slow and manageable pace, you have to be clear about what ideas you want to show and how you want to use the media elements to convey them and then be willing to allow your students to surpass your technical knowledge. Finally, keep yourself focused on what you do best: facilitating student learning in your content area. Remembering your particular area of expertise makes it easier to become an apprentice in another.

3

Making a Real-World Connection

Curriculum, multimedia, real-world connection, assessment, collaboration, extended time, and student decision making—seven dimensions of project-based multimedia projects may seem to be a lot to think about; but if you have a multimedia project with a strong *real-world connection*, you can hardly go wrong. Student engagement is just about guaranteed. This is a project your students will work hard on now and remember for a long time.

Multimedia is like any other practical art form—it makes sense only when it is part of a context. In wood shop, students don't make joints, they make birdhouses with joints. In sewing, they don't make seams, they make clothing with seams. We don't just combine random media elements, we make multimedia that communicates something. In creating a real-world connection, you are embedding multimedia in a rich context in which students will learn and practice skills, gather and present information, and solve problems. Indeed,

Finding real-world connections to student projects is largely a matter of perception. To an adult, the "real world" is work and economics. To a kid, the "real world" is the playground when the supervisor is looking the other way.

—ELEMENTARY TEACHER

the real-world connection is a strong distinguishing element of this learning approach that makes it so motivating for students.

A real-world connection means that students see a reason to do this project, other than the fact that you assigned it and they will get a grade on it. There are so many ways to connect to the real world that even beginners to the multimedia approach can design a project that students will find worthwhile.

To connect to the real world, you don't even have to leave your school—it is also part of the real world, and a big part of the students' real world. Of course, if you want to connect outside the school walls, technology makes it easier than ever before. Your students can e-mail subject matter experts and use the Internet to find primary source data.

A Real-World Connection: One Example

At Gunn High School in Palo Alto, California, Spanish is the language spoken by many of the immigrant students. For students who were learning Spanish, their Spanish language skills gave them a special ability to communicate with these immigrants. They wrote and produced a video for new Spanish-speaking students to orient them to the school. The students could see that the school really needed this video and that they were the ones to produce it. In making the video, they had a reason to strive for perfect grammar and pronunciation. They suddenly needed lots of vocabulary words, some not found in their textbooks.

This project connects to the real world in many ways. It connects to a real audience—the Spanish-speaking students. It fulfills a real need—the school's need to welcome these immigrant students. It connects to student interests—students could choose an area of the school to describe in the video. It applies students' special talents and skills—particularly the ability to speak and write Spanish—to a real-world purpose.

Ten Kinds of Real-World Connections

As the example illustrates, there are many ways to connect to the real world, and a given project can connect in more than one way. To get you started, here are 10 ways you can connect to the real world with your students. As you read these examples, you'll think of even more.

Our 10 real-world connection ideas are organized into three categories. First, students can connect to the real world through their project topics. That is, the topics themselves involve some expression of students' lives and identities. Second, students can connect through authentic interactions with people and institutions within and outside school. Third, students connect through creating a presentation that helps them imagine or achieve a future goal.

Connecting Through Project Topics

1. Connecting through student interests. This is one of the easiest ways to connect to the real world—ask students to create a presentation to share their knowledge about a topic they care about. Examples of this kind of project include a "math in the real world" presentation, in which students show how math is involved in their favorite hobbies and sports. Another example is a science fair presentation, in which students design and conduct experiments about a question of their own choosing and present the results in multimedia. You will get to know your students in a new way and find out about their out-of-school passions. We need to keep two things in mind when connecting to student interests. First, even a project about the physics of skiing is still just a flashy physics report. Connecting through student interests works best when your project is interactive (see section "Connecting Through Interaction"). For example, share that skiing presentation at a meeting of the school ski club, and include information about how knowing the physics can help you ski better or select better equipment.

The second thing to remember when connecting to student interests is making sure the project meets your curricular goals within the student presentations. Some subject areas are easier than others to relate to student interests. If you teach medieval French poetry, connecting to student interests might not be your best route to the real world. Read on—we've got nine other strategies.

2. Connecting through student experiences. With this strategy, you ask students to bring their unique experiences and perspectives into a project. For example, one high school teacher's English-as-a-Second Language (ESL) students were all born in other countries. They were especially well qualified to teach the rest of the student body a thing or two about culture in their native lands. Each student chose three aspects of culture such as music, dance, or religion. Students created a hypermedia presentation for the school library that showcased the many cultures represented in just one ESL class. Students were able to teach other students about a favorite French rock star, show how Afghan culture was affected by war, and provide countless other insider's perspectives.

If your students' experiences aren't quite right for bringing your curricular goals to life, you can create the experiences you need. For example, one elementary schoolteacher built a multimedia project out of a field trip to Point Reyes National Seashore and the California Academy of Sciences. Students brought their experiences on the field trip into the design of a presentation about Point Reyes habitats.

3. Connecting through significant issues. Many topics in the real world are particularly compelling to young people. These topics include public health, racism, poverty, and the power of the media. Students respond to these topics because they may be personally affected by them, because they are often passionate about fairness and equity, or because they can try to effect change.

These topics are particularly germane to math, science, and social studies curriculums. For example, students can create powerful media presentations that mix statistical analyses and science concepts related to drug abuse, with interview clips about the effects of drug abuse in local people's lives.

One middle school teacher used this approach to bring her social studies unit on immigration to life. Immigration is a topic that affects all her students in one way or another. She asked students to interview their relatives about how their families came to America. They collected artifacts such as photographs and medals and created a Web site that included the artifacts and stories. Many of the students had never heard the stories before because relatives found them painful to talk about.

I'm not talking about inane "story problems" in which students figure out at what geographical point two airplanes will cross each other given starting points and flight speed. Nor am I talking about contrived simulations. What I now do with students is involve them in projects that make a difference in the lives of people and/or involve important research—real research, not just rediscovering someone else's research.

—TECHNOLOGY LEARNING
COORDINATOR

Connecting Through Interaction

4. *Improving the real world.* Nothing is more empowering to kids than changing the big bad grown-up world, unless perhaps it's changing their own kid world. Your students have had plenty of opportunity to be influenced by media—turn the tables and give them their own turn to use media to influence others and effect change. Is there a local political issue your students can get involved in? Almost any issue has good curricular ties—environmental issues to science, for example. Students can research the issue and make a multimedia presentation for the city council or their congressional representative, or they can air their presentations on public access cable. Students don't even have to agree—they can create multiple presentations promoting differing points of view. Students will be amazed that they can use music, video, and compelling graphic images to convince others, just as professionals do. You will be amazed at how much technique students have picked up just by living in a media-rich world.

Opportunities to improve the world abound, even within school. Ask students what issues most affect their lives. From drugs and violence to excessive homework, students can use media to convince others that change is a good idea.

5. *Relating to clients.* When you give students a chance to engage in a professional relationship with real clients, you are teaching them useful real-world skills. These include defining and working with clients' design requirements; matching their style and addressing their audience; listening and responding to client feedback; and working within clients' time constraints.

Your students' product can be as simple as a Web site for parents to keep them up to date on the goings-on in the classroom. In some schools, students design Web pages for businesses and individuals. Is there a charity near you that needs a video or Web page promoting its work? How about a professional society in your subject area? Maybe they would like some student-produced Web pages to add to their site that explore a particular subject matter. Clients can also be other students in real or simulated situations, as when students in one class designed dream houses for "clients" in another class.

6. Interacting with assessors. With all the talk about raising standards, what could be better than giving your students the opportunity to learn about standards for professional-quality work? A few minutes with a professional designer or content expert can pay great dividends in inspiring students to work to professional levels.

One middle school teacher asked professional graphic designers to critique her students' work. The designers used student work as a starting point to discuss graphic design concepts, such as how layout could show the connections among media elements. The students used the critique to develop their own rubric for evaluating their next product.

You can also bring in content experts to assess your students' work. For instance, if you are making a presentation about a local environmental issue, students would benefit from the opportunity to present their work in progress to one or more environmental scientists. An environmental scientist might be found through local universities, the city planning department, and local environmental consulting companies. Students will learn more than just subject matter—you can explore possible biases the expert might have.

Real-world assessors can be design or subject experts, and they can also be clients or potential users of your students' work. For example, if your class is making a presentation to teach some content to younger students, ask students from the target age range to come and use the product. Your students can find out if the younger students can understand the information and use the product successfully.

One more way for students to interact with assessors is to submit projects to multimedia fairs and competitions. Students can get valuable feedback from judges and see how their work stacks up against other projects in the competition.

7. Interacting with people who know. Do you want your project to do more than reproduce information on other Web sites? Students can get original content for their presentations by conducting their own interviews with people who have a perspective on students' topics.

One high school teacher's students created content for their World War II presentations by interviewing older relatives and friends who remembered World War II. Besides taping the interviews, they also photographed memorabilia their interviewees had saved, such as a handkerchief given to a husband as he went off to war. They even asked an interviewee to teach a student his favorite song from the era, and their recording of the student and the man singing the song together is one of the most moving parts of the presentation. The project as a whole created new knowledge—knowledge that had never before been compiled or organized anywhere.

Connecting to the Future

8. Learning adult work and life skills. All multimedia projects connect in this way because creating multimedia *is* an adult work skill; so is planning a big project, working in teams, and organizing information. In fact, students in video and multimedia production classes often take their skills into the professional arena even before graduation.

Many subject areas connect easily to adult work. Students in one high school class learned skills related to financial management by creating their own (pretend) "mini mutual funds." They researched stocks, created portfolios, and followed their investments for eight weeks. They created multimedia presentations to promote their mutual funds.

Life outside of work is also fertile ground for project ideas of this type. One teacher's high school students researched a car they wanted to buy. They created a multimedia presentation showing price comparisons, financing options, and insurance costs.

9. Creating a body of work. Students, particularly in upper grade levels, can create multimedia portfolios of their own work. The portfolio can showcase their multimedia production skills or mastery of other art or professional skills. It can also be a personal Web page that acts as a resume. Students can submit their portfolios to competitions or as part of applications to undergraduate and professional programs, internships, and jobs. It is easy for students to see how such a project connects directly to their futures.

10. Creating images of the future. Students research and create multimedia presentations that help them envision their futures. For example, one

Indeed, the finished project was stunning. It was entered into a video contest for young movie makers sponsored by a local museum and won honorable mention. All four students were honored at the museum and their movie was shown on the big screen. The team members unanimously decided to give the trophy that was presented to them to Garth, the director. After he received the trophy, Garth said to me, "This is the start of my career in filmmaking!"

—MIDDLE SCHOOL TEACHER

high school teacher's students created a "Careers" Web site. The site included information about careers that the students wanted to research, including information about the local labor market and job search tips. A colleague's students created presentations about careers in art. Each group selected one career in art to explore. Their research included interviews with practitioners in the community. The groups then created multimedia presentations about the career.

Finding a Real-World Connection

As you can see, you and your students can connect to the real world in many ways. Finding the connections that make sense for you depends on many factors, including your curriculum, the issues and potential audiences around you, and the time you have available.

For example, suppose your subject is 7th grade social studies and your curriculum is world history. Your year is packed full, so you want to spend no more than four weeks of class time on your project. What kinds of real-world connections make the most sense?

Connecting to existing student interests is possible but may be difficult. Can students research the origins of a favorite hobby or sport in the times and cultures you study? Depending on your students, this connection may be a stretch.

Perhaps the simplest connection would be a "Traces of History" presentation, where groups of students find, photograph, and record historical allusions or elements in your town or neighborhood. Students might photograph buildings and public artifacts that draw from previous historical periods, like an ancient Greek facade, or a Ming-style vase in the local Chinese restaurant, and then look for patterns around town to see which historical periods are represented where. They may decide to create a multimedia map of town, or a section of town, which shows these patterns and explains their historical origins. Finding a real audience would make the project more significant. Perhaps the local chamber of commerce or visitors' center would like to display the project.

Connections between your curriculum and significant issues are a possibility. Students could select an issue of interest, or you could choose one for which you have good resources. For example, how have different cultures handled poverty or homelessness in their societies? Students could create a presentation for either state government officials or groups that advocate for better living conditions. The message of the presentation could be that history can shed light on our current solutions. Are there ideas in history that we should revive now? Does history show us that our current solutions are actually throwbacks to medieval times? The main drawback of this kind of connection could be time: in four weeks, can students do enough research to do a reasonable treatment of the issue? You would have to make sure that topics were narrow and focused enough for the time available and that as many resources as possible were ready to go at the start of the project.

Possibilities for interactive connections abound, depending somewhat on where you live and what resources are easily available. If you choose a "significant issue" topic and live in a university town, perhaps graduate-level history students would critique your students' work. Taking a different direction, if there are people in your town from one of the countries you study, could they help you compare how the same historical period you teach is taught in their country? Students could learn a lot about how our culture influences our perspectives on history. Relating to clients is less likely, particularly given your time frame, but possible. Is there a teacher who would like a certain kind of multimedia resource for teaching world history? Could a local historical society or museum use a media exhibit on one of your curriculum topics?

Finally, you could connect to adult work—the most obvious connection is to the work of an adult historian. Perhaps a historian from a local museum, historical society, or university could help get students involved in a small piece of historical research that could culminate in a multimedia presentation about the results. This example shows only one of many ways you might think through the possible real-world connections for a curriculum area.

4

Defining and Planning a Multimedia Learning Project

So you've read this far, and you say to yourself, "Yes, project-based multimedia learning is a good thing. It's pedagogically sound. It's motivating for kids. It's the wave of the future. I'm ready to dive in. Where do I start?"

The answer to that question depends on you and your working style. When you clean your house, how do you go about it? Do you thoroughly clean one room at a time, finishing it before moving on to the next? Do you prefer to putter about among rooms, picking up something here, polishing something there, until finally the whole house is tidy? Either approach will work in planning your unit. It doesn't matter whether you start in the kitchen or the den, whether you first vacuum or wash the windows. What matters is that you know what needs to be done and, before you collapse on the sofa, you've done it. It's the same with planning project-based multimedia units. The *Project-Based Learning with Multimedia* CD-ROM (available from the Association for Supervision and Curriculum Development) includes a convenient

Teachers from the Challenge 2000 Multimedia Project were encouraged to form partnerships, and when it was all over, 95 percent of participating teachers said they wanted to continue the partnership next year. As a middle school teacher explained, "Doing these types of projects is fun but also stressful. It is helpful to have someone else going through it at the same time. It also helps to see the range of projects that come from a wider range of students."

A high school teacher agrees: "Two or three heads are better than one. Working together was an enriching experience especially since there was some overlapping of students. We built on the experience our students had in one another's classes. It was easy to see these students become the class experts. We teachers provided moral and technical support to one another as we watched the creative chaos we had created."

planning tool that can help you. As you plan, consider the questions that follow.

What Do I Need to Teach?

Though a few of us may work in liberal or "free" schools with the leeway to teach whatever we wish, most of us are charged with "delivering" a required curriculum of some sort. These go by many names: standards, learning outcomes, frameworks, course syllabi, and district curricula. In one district, we heard teachers talking about "ESLRs" (pronounced EHSlurs). When we asked, we learned that meant Essential Learning Results. A rose is a rose is a rose. . . . Whatever they're called in our local context, we ignore them at our peril. To the extent that they are well crafted and well chosen, we ignore them at our students' peril as well.

More often than not, those who wrote our curricula were overly optimistic about what one human can teach in one course, semester, or grade. Happily, one of the powerful things about a well-designed multimedia unit is that it can bundle quite a few skill and knowledge objectives into one highly motivating activity. Early in your planning, take a good look at your required curriculum. Do not go forward with any project until you can specifically identify the required learning outcomes that the project will address.

What Equipment Do I Have Available?

There's no point in planning a video project if you don't have a video camera. Take an inventory of the equipment available for the project. What do you have in your own classroom? What does the teacher next door have that he isn't using? What's available for checking out in your school? Does your district media center have things to lend? Does your local computer-using educators association have an equipment loan program? Don't overlook your students. How many of them have computers at home? Video cameras? Scanners? A Zip drive? Before you finish planning your unit, know what tools are at hand for doing the job.

Also, check the age of your computers—multimedia requires fairly up-to-date machines with ample memory and disk space. These requirements vary with the software you choose and the nature of your project. You can get a quick estimate from software manuals, which specify requirements for computers, operating systems, and memory.

What Applications Do I Have Available?

The Boston Pops needs a score. The Royal Shakespeare Company needs a script. Your computer needs applications or it can't do anything. You probably have a word processing program and a spreadsheet. With these you can produce text, figures, charts, graphs, and—using their clip art collections—even some pictures. You'll need a multimedia authoring program. Depending on the complexity and sophistication of your project, you may want additional applications. Turn on your computer and see what's there. Be sure to check each one. As you check, note the versions as well. You can save yourself grief by ensuring that all the applications your students use are the same version. The bottom line here is to *be realistic*. If you can only provide a bucket and a spade, challenge your students to build a beautiful sandcastle. Leave the skyscraper for later.

What Is the Project?

For some teachers, especially those with experience teaching a particular class or grade level and familiarity with the project approach, project ideas seem to jump out of the blue. It's as if they have a matchmaker program running in the background, constantly scanning the environment and comparing potential projects with their curricular needs. For such teachers, the challenge is to select one from among many competing candidates.

On the other hand, if you're a teacher who is new to a subject or grade level, or trying project-based learning for the first time, you may have to be more deliberate in searching for a project.

If you are trying multimedia production for the first time, you may want to select a topic with which you feel very comfortable. Already knowing something about the topic will reduce the number of new variables and allow you to have expertise in at least one aspect of the learning environment. Knowing something about the topic allows room for you to learn a lot about technology and its management without having the extra pressure of acquiring massive amounts of content knowledge, too. In choosing a familiar topic, make sure that there are opportunities for your students to do primary investigations. The collection of primary resources and experiences adds excitement to the project-based multimedia experience.

Topics that give students the opportunity to collect primary resources call for real organization. It is easiest to start with a single class topic from which groups can select subtopics. Once you have tried this a few times and really have a handle on the multimedia production process, then branch out to several class topics or to an array of self-selected group topics.

You can find many other sources for project ideas. Take a look at the local newspaper. What's going on in your town that clearly affects your students? What are the issues and debates in the community? Is the city council arguing about whether or not to enlarge the airport? Are local factories exceeding smog control limits? Are skateboarders being evicted from the local shopping mall? Is the school board considering changing graduation requirements?

Fellow teachers are another good source. Who else does projects in your school or district? Ask around. See what people are up to. Explain that you're looking for a project to teach such-and-such content. Don't limit your search to your immediate vicinity. Check the Internet. Organizations such as Global SchoolNet Foundation and National School Network offer projects to teachers everywhere. Some of these cost money, but many are free of charge. Contact your local service clubs such as Kiwanis, Rotary, and Lions. Their national organizations publish annual handbooks with many suggestions for service projects. You may find a project, an ally, and even financial support all in one place. Finally, be sure to attend conferences and meetings sponsored by the various professional organizations, such as the Association for Supervision and Curriculum Development (ASCD), Computer Using Educators (CUE), and the International Society for Technology in Education (ISTE).

In all likelihood, you'll end up with a list of potential projects from which to select. In making your choice, test the project ideas against all the other considerations listed here and especially against your curriculum requirements. Be sure that the project you select has a good "cost-benefit ratio"; that is, for the time, energy, and resources you will invest, the learning outcomes will be many and important.

What Multimedia Product Will the Students Create?

In project-based multimedia learning, the students' experience culminates in the creation of a multimedia product. It may be as simple as a linear slide show to support an oral presentation or as complex as a large, interactive Web site. Perhaps you had some idea of your multimedia product when you first conceptualized your project. Or you may have first come upon a particularly compelling topic or issue and are now ready to consider what sort of multimedia product will best serve your learning goals. Either way, now is the time to decide, at least tentatively, what your students will produce. In making this decision, keep in mind your required curriculum and your inventory of multimedia equipment and applications. Will making this product increase the likelihood that your students learn what you want them to learn? Is it feasible given the equipment, software, and other technical resources at hand? Yes? Then you're ready to proceed.

In making the final decision about what form the multimedia project should take—and this is, by the way, a wonderful opportunity to involve your students in decision making—consider the strengths of the different forms relative to your project's goal. Oil painting probably serves better than watercolor for rendering fine detail. A stage play might work better than a motion picture for telling a story that takes place completely within one room of a house. Likewise, one form of multimedia can serve a given purpose better than another. Figure 4.1 gives you some guidance about the strengths of some common multimedia forms.

Form of Multimedia	Works well...
Video	• When you want to tell a story. • When you want to demonstrate something.
Linear computer presentation (that is, each slide or screen leads only to the next)	• When you want to control the user's path through material. • When you want the user to see and hear only certain information in a fixed order.
Web site or hypermedia stack	When you want to offer a range of information and grant freedom for users to encounter the information in their own self-chosen sequence.

FIGURE 4.1. STRENGTHS OF DIFFERENT MULTIMEDIA FORMS

Can I Put It in a Nutshell?

Though it's certainly not required, we strongly urge you to stop at this point and describe your project in 40 words or less. Imagine that your project is a television show and you've got to write a short entry for *TV Guide*. Sound silly? Not really. In business, it's called an "elevator speech" and any salesperson or would-be entrepreneur must have one. By forcing yourself to write an abstract that succinctly states the essence of the project, you will focus your concept and thereby increase the chances you and your students will have a satisfying experience. You'll also have a great tool to use when communicating to parents and explaining your project to your principal.

What Are My Goals and Objectives?

To start searching for a project, you only need a general grasp of your curriculum. Before you settle on a project, be certain you've identified specific goals and objectives and that you're convinced the project will address them effectively. Depending on how—and how well—your local curriculum is written, you may be able to simply copy what you need directly into your unit plan. This is especially helpful in creating your goals, which are general statements such as "Students know that cells function similarly in all living organisms."

Objectives are another matter. They need to get down to the nitty-gritty and tell exactly how you are going to measure whether or not your students reach the lofty goals you set. Objectives define the evidence you'll accept that proves students learned what you wanted them to learn. Truly measurable objectives can be hard to write. Perhaps that's the reason they are often absent from curriculum guides or omitted in lesson planning. Ideally, for each major goal you have set, you'll determine at least one concrete, measurable objective. Figure 4.2 shows some examples of goals and objectives from multimedia projects.

How Much Time Shall We Spend on This?

Some teachers launch a project the first day of school and continue it for most of the year. Some teachers wait until they've had a chance to "train" their students and establish classroom routines. Others prefer to save

FIGURE 4.2. EXAMPLES OF GOALS/STANDARDS STATEMENTS AND INSTRUCTIONAL OBJECTIVES

Examples of Goals/Standards	Examples of Instructional Objectives
9th Grade Science Students will understand Newton's laws of motion.	In groups of three, students will create a multimedia presentation that uses animation to accurately illustrate one of Newton's laws of motion. After viewing presentations created by their classmates, other students will identify the law illustrated with 90 percent accuracy.
5th Grade Mathematics Students will use a variety of methods, such as words, numbers, symbols, charts, graphs, tables, diagrams, and models to explain mathematical reasoning.	Working with a partner, students will develop a narrated PowerPoint presentation that explains why a given algorithm "works" (for example, algorithms for finding the lowest common denominator, dividing fractions, calculating area, or long division). Presentations will be viewed and scored by students from another class of the same grade using a 4-point scoring rubric adapted for this project. The average score for all presentations will be 3 or higher and no presentation will score below 2.
2nd Grade Social Studies and Language Arts Students will • Differentiate between those things that happened long ago and yesterday by tracing the history of a family through the use of primary and secondary sources, including artifacts, photographs, interviews, and documents. • Group related ideas and maintain a consistent focus. • Revise original drafts to improve sequence and provide more descriptive detail.	Working as one large collaborative group under the teacher's direction, students will select a notable local family for study and create a multimedia presentation that tells that family's story through at least three generations. The presentation will be viewed and scored by a committee of seven adults from the community using a 5-point scoring rubric. The presentation will earn an average score of at least 3.8 and no single score below 3. *Note:* Goals are drawn from California State Content Standards.

projects for the second half of the year when student motivation may be waning and classroom life needs a shot of adrenaline. In any case, you need to be realistic about how much time the project will take compared to how much time truly is available. Think about the other things that will be going on at the same time as the project. Will your class be shoving off on a weeklong field trip to outdoor education camp? Will all work come to a standstill while everyone takes state achievement tests? Will all the athletes in your class be missing project work time in order to travel to their "away" games? Every teacher we've worked with says their first projects took longer than they had anticipated. You'll increase your chances of success—and reduce your stress level—if you think through your project thoroughly and add a couple of extra weeks to your schedule for unanticipated delays.

How Will I Involve Students in Decision Making?

As you conceptualize and define your unit, think about how you might involve your students in key decisions. One of the strengths of project-based learning is its potential for developing many cognitive, affective, and social skills at once. To realize this potential, teachers need to let the reins out a bit and give students a degree of control over important aspects of the work. One simple way to do this is to list all the decisions that must be made between the day you start the unit and the day you end it. When you finish, go over the list and ask yourself, "Which of these decisions requires my professional judgment alone? Which might I make in consultation with my students? Which ones could I leave up to my students alone?" Next to each decision write "me," "us," or "students." Depending on your comfort level, you may choose to defer some of these decisions until later in the process. You may even include your students in *deciding* who decides!

One approach to involving students in decision making deserves special attention: the class meeting. (If you are new to class meetings, read the chapter on them in William Glasser's classic *Schools Without Failure*, 1975.) Use this method for high-level, important decisions that will affect all parties, not just a few individuals. Explain the situation to your students. Let them know what needs to be decided and, if it's not obvious, why you chose to give them a role in making the decision. Describe any constraints. Share the alternatives as you see them. Invite the students to suggest others. Then, lead the class in a discussion of the pros and cons of the various alternatives. Finally, make the decision.

When involving your whole class in making a decision, a few caveats are in order. At the outset, make the parameters and procedure explicit. Are some alternatives off the table? Are you asking for the students' advice prior to making the decision yourself, or are you truly leaving the decision to them? What mechanism will be used for the final decision? Majority vote? Consensus? Will you play it safe and reserve veto power? Be clear on these things in your own mind, and make them equally clear to your students. This will ensure that your students have an empowering experience rather than one that engenders disappointment and skepticism.

What Forms of Collaboration Will I Include?

As we discussed in Chapter 1, project-based multimedia learning is *collaborative*—each student's contributions affect the final product. You want to set up working arrangements that will enable students to share their knowledge and

In one elementary school project, "The 24 Views of the Ohlone Structure" (inspired by Japanese painter Hokusai's *36 Views of Mt. Fuji*), each student was to produce his or her own "view" of a single school object or area through artwork and poetry. The students toured the school and came up with two possibilities: the play structure and the school farm. They held a class meeting to decide which one to choose. It was an ideal decision for a class meeting because the outcome affected everyone, and the discussion helped everyone become familiar with useful features of the chosen object.

The students found several advantages in choosing the play structure over the farm. The structure had interesting geometric shapes that would inspire the artwork. The structure was more bounded; the farm was so big that viewers would not necessarily know they were looking at 24 views of the same place. Several students related this discussion to researchers, providing evidence that one of the reasons for the decision was shared class knowledge. See the finished project at http://pblmm.k12.ca.us.

The project that my students worked on was structured so that they all contributed elements to one large presentation. The goal of each class was to create a 12- to 15-minute animated video that included many of the important concepts covered in 6th grade math. A time traveler went from place to place and observed or participated in the solution to a challenging math problem representing one of the topics. Students in each class worked in groups of three and were responsible for a one-minute animated video on their topic. A group of student directors was in charge of the introductory and ending scenes as well as the transition scenes from one group to another.

—MIDDLE SCHOOL TEACHER

skills and to build on one another's strengths. You want a structure that facilitates synergy. Ultimately, you want your students to create a final product that would have been impossible without the combined contributions of their hands, hearts, and brains.

Collaboration can take simple or complex forms. At the simple end of the continuum, you might have individual students contribute cards to a hypermedia stack or pages to a Web site. Such an approach would represent collaboration to the extent that individual students' contributions drew on their strengths and reflected their own talents and interests. In contrast, it would be harder to claim collaboration for a cookie-cutter approach in which each student completes an identical template you prepared. At a more complex level, you might assign partners and have each pair responsible for contributing to the larger project. Or you might have students work in small groups, either to contribute to a larger project or to separate, stand-alone projects.

Here it's important to mention the interplay between student decision making and collaboration. When students are involved in decision making—especially if they have a say over key aspects of the project—the chances of collaboration are multiplied. Imagine a group of students debating how to proceed with some important aspect of the work. Finally, they come to a decision based on everyone's input and deliberation. Almost by definition, work that is shaped by such a process is collaborative.

What Resources Will I Need?

For a rich learning experience, you and your students will want to consult many resources. Just what these will be depends on the nature of the project and the topics under study. The main thing is to think ahead about the kinds of resources you want to have available. By planning ahead you can increase the chances that materials will be available when you need them. The following are some general categories of resources to consider.

Library Materials

Despite the advent of the Internet, the old-fashioned library is certainly not outdated. Computerized catalogs can help you quickly identify materials in your school or local public library related to what your students will be studying. Enlist the aid of the library reference staff to help you find materials and to ensure that materials are available when your students need them. If there is a high demand for certain items, your librarian can request additional copies from other library branches or place materials on reserve. If nothing else, alert the librarian ahead of time to your students' possible topics so he can plan ahead.

Field Trips

What information can your students collect or what resources can they gather by leaving school and going out into the community? Do nearby museums or other organizations have special collections of information or resources about your students' topics? Are there places your students need to visit to gather firsthand knowledge? Don't assume that every field trip requires a bus. Depending on what you are studying and the logistics of your community, you may even be able to access relevant resources through a walking field trip in the vicinity of your school. Another alternative is to divide up the fieldwork among the students. For example, together you could make a list of places to visit and information to gather. Individuals or small groups of students would be responsible for each "assignment." One elementary school class writing a school history used this approach.

People as Resources

Chances are that people in your community will have special knowledge or experience in the area your students are studying. Identify them and find a way to tap their expertise as resources. You may invite them to your class for your students to interview or to give a lecture or demonstration. Your whole class or a small group of students may interview some people where they work or live and report back to the class.

The Internet

The Internet provides virtual access to a growing variety of resources. As search engines become more sophisticated, it is easier to find relevant sites for a given topic or to answer a given question. You'll need to plan around your school's Internet "Acceptable Use Policy." You may want to do a presearch and select a limited set of reference sites, or you may want students to search the Internet themselves. Either way, be sure to spend time talking about how to judge the veracity and accuracy of information gathered from the Internet as well as from other sources.

News Media

Don't overlook newspapers, television, and radio as sources of information. You may assign different students to monitor different information channels during the course of the project. For example, some students might have the responsibility of skimming different newspapers. Other students might regularly check television program listings, and other students might do likewise for radio programs. Sometimes a simple telephone call to a television or radio station programming department can provide information about upcoming programs so you can plan ahead for listening or taping. Many stations also post their upcoming programming on their Web sites. Internet-savvy students might want to use some of the news-gathering services on the Internet, which they can tailor to search for stories according to customized search terms.

Original Research

Depending on what your students' project involves, you may want to have them do some original research. This might take the form of conducting experiments, doing surveys, interviewing, or preparing their own case studies.

How Will I Measure What Students Learn?

Measuring educational accomplishment is a complex and difficult task. Entire college textbooks have been written on the subject. (A particularly good one is W. James Popham's *Classroom Assessment: What Teachers Need to Know*, 1998. An entire chapter is devoted to the topic of assessment in this book.) The point here is simply to remember to plan ahead for how to measure at least some of the key learning outcomes the project was designed to reach. If the project is to add to the student's store of knowledge, how will that knowledge be measured? If students will be developing skills, how will the growth of these skills be determined? If you're hoping students will change attitudes or develop values, how will you document they have done so?

Look back at the objectives you wrote previously. Try to identify at least one measure for each of your two or three most important objectives. For example, if one of your objectives has to do with content knowledge, consider what test might measure what you are after. If you are expecting that the students will develop skills, is there an observation checklist that you might employ for rating their skill level at different stages of the project? Just because you are working with new technology or a new instructional model, don't ignore traditional methods of classroom measurement, such as multiple choice, "true and false" and essay tests, surveys, questionnaires, and the like.

One of the most important things to do is to establish baseline data before students begin work on the project. If you anticipate growth in knowledge, choose or develop a test of that knowledge and give it to your students before the project as a pretest. Give it again at the end as a post-test. If you are focusing on skill development, have your students perform one or more of the tasks involved and rate their skill level before the project begins. Then do the same thing when the project ends. Even if your measures are not sensitive enough to show fine differences in individual student growth, at least make sure you can determine the proportion of your class that can meet a given criteria before the project begins and how that proportion has increased when the project ends.

One way to be certain you have chosen workable measures is to construct a simple graph or pie chart with hypothetical data. Predict how your students will score on your pretest and, if they make the growth you hope for, on your post-test. Plot the scores on your graph. Label the axes. For example, Figure 4.3 shows how a teacher might hope a class would improve after completing three different multimedia projects over the course of a school year. Show your graph to a friend and ask for feedback. If you can't create a graph or chart that makes sense to both you and your friend, chances are that you have not yet completely figured out how you will measure your students' growth.

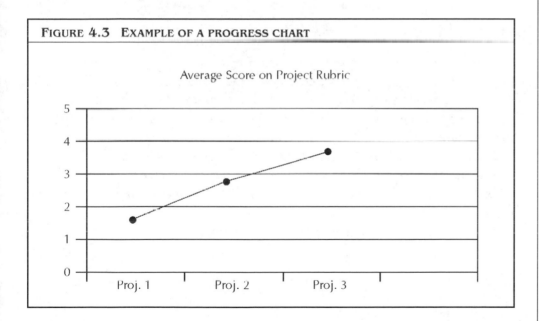

FIGURE 4.3   EXAMPLE OF A PROGRESS CHART

Average Score on Project Rubric

What's the Real-World Connection?

As your initial planning process concludes, reflect on the real-world aspects of the project. How does it relate to the lives of your students? How well do the project's activities mirror important activities in the world outside of school? Will the students' products be useful to others? Will your students see the connection between what they are doing and the real world? Look critically at what you have planned and see if there are ways you can tighten or strengthen the connection and make it more tangible.

What's My Own Life Like Right Now?

Before you set your plan in concrete, test it against your *own* real world! You have conceptualized and designed an exciting, challenging learning project for your students. Can you pull it off? What competing demands will you face? Are you taking classes at night for your master's degree? Are you trying to raise a family and teach at the same time? How's your health and stamina? The point is *be realistic*. Teachers find project-based multimedia learning exhilarating but also exhausting. If you're starting to have second thoughts, consider reducing the scope or complexity of the project. Don't give it up— just simplify it. You want to plan for success, and that means keeping your own needs in mind, as well as those of your students.

5

Ready, Set, Go!

By now, you have defined your project, gathered resources, maybe even scheduled three weeks of time in the computer lab for next month. What to do next?

Every project is different so we can't tell you how yours should progress. Still, in watching teachers and students produce hundreds of multimedia projects, we have noticed a few things about how projects often unfold. What follows is not a prescription but a set of suggestions based on our observations. Our goal is to help you, particularly if you're a first-timer, plan out the events and timing of your project. The time estimates depend greatly on the project's complexity. For a short presentation involving one or two screens of content per student or group, use the lower estimates. For presentations involving substantial content or a complex branching structure (many menus and hyperlinks), use the higher estimates. Overall, a simple project will take three to four weeks, and a complex project can easily extend over much of the school year (but you probably won't work on it every day). Figure 5.1 provides an overview of the stages of a typical project.

FIGURE 5.1 OVERVIEW OF A TYPICAL PROJECT

Stage	Estimated Time
Before the project starts	2 weeks
Introducing the project	1–2 days
Learning the technology	1–3 days
Preliminary research and planning	3 days–3 weeks
Concept design and storyboarding	3–5 days
First draft production	1–3 weeks
Assessing, testing, and finalizing presentations	1–3 weeks
Concluding activities	1–3 days
Total class time	5–13 weeks

Although even five weeks is significant class time to devote to a project, many teachers have found ways to trim the time a little and to attend to other responsibilities during the project, as follows:

• ***Use technology students already know.*** This cuts the technology learning time, production time, and rework time.

- **Use time outside of class wherever possible.** Older students can conduct much of their preliminary research as homework.
- **Run a "skills track" as homework.** Math teachers in particular assign skills practice as homework in multimedia projects. The skills may be unrelated to the multimedia project, but students can continue to make progress on them while the project is going on.
- **Use "special" classes (like art or music) as extra time.** Can students work on the design and composition of their project in art class? Can they compose or critique background music in their music class? This is a chance to collaborate with other teachers and gain their subject area perspectives.
- **Increase planning time.** Though it may seem paradoxical, actual production goes quite fast if students compose text and select and prepare graphics and sounds as they plan.

Before the Project Starts (Two Weeks of Intermittent Work)

Doing the following things before the project starts will have big payoffs in time saved and project satisfaction.

Create Project Description and Milestones

The description should include your nutshell description of the project (see Chapter 4) and your instructional goals and objectives. Also include a list of the project components students will be responsible for and their due dates. Without deadlines, your project will become the monster that ate your school year.

Create a Parent Letter

Your students will talk about your project at home, so make sure parents understand how the project is instructionally valuable. Also ask for any help you think parents can provide. Figure 5.2 is a sample parent letter.

FIGURE 5.2 SAMPLE PARENT LETTER

Dear Parents,

For the next six weeks, your child will be working on a multimedia project in math class called Designing a Dream House. Students will work in small groups to design homes for fictional clients, and prepare multimedia presentations about their designs. The project develops and deepens students' understanding of many math topics from our curriculum, including area, volume, proportion, functions, and applications of math to the real world. The project also addresses several of our district technology standards for this year.

We will be using PowerPoint to create the presentations, and need parent volunteers to help students stay productive with the software during class. If you know PowerPoint and can volunteer during even one class period, please contact me.

We would also like to have a professional architect assess student designs. Contact me if you can help or know someone who can.

Sincerely,

Mrs. Murphy

Work with Real-World Connections

If you have people outside the classroom involved as clients or assessors, work with them to make an appropriate schedule and include their ideas for activities.

Prepare Resources

Work with your school media specialist to pull relevant books from the school library and to create bookmarks to useful Web sites. You can also create a quick reference that reminds students how to do common tasks on the computer.

Prepare Software and Peripherals

Work with school or district technical support to install and connect cameras, microphones, scanners, or any other peripherals you anticipate using. Go through the entire process of, for example, scanning a picture and putting it into a Web page to make sure it all works.

Organize Computer Files

Set up an organization for computer files and backups. This one is really important and will save you and your students hours of frustration and rework. Naming files and folders after their file type and section title helps to keep things organized and makes it easier to merge elements later on. For example, if the class topic is "World War II as Seen Through Local Eyes," and the presentation is subdivided into "The Home Front," "Soldiers in Combat," and "World Events," then these subcategories become the names of folders that are created on each computer. Within each folder, there should be other folders for different file formats such as images, text, movies, and sound. Depending on the production's complexity, you may want to create folders for subtopics, as well. Figure 5.3 shows a sample filing system.

Finding files is one of the biggest time drains for student producers. Setting up a systematic naming system in advance saves a lot of time. Having the same naming protocol on each computer will simplify the search for materials. It also sets up an easy system for preparing the files for authoring. In setting up your naming system, try to get advice from someone experienced in working with both Mac and Windows operating systems to avoid pitfalls caused by their differing file-naming conventions. If you're composing on Macs, for example, by adding Windows ".***" suffixes to your file names, you can increase the chances that you'll be able to run your presentation on both Mac and Windows machines.

Dividing folders by file types has an additional advantage. Each file type requires a specific way of preparing it for the authoring stage. Text files need spell checking and conversion to a universal file format like "html" or simple text. Media files need to be optimized and converted to universal file formats like jpeg or mov. Placing similar file types in common folders makes it easy to give quick whole-class or small-group demonstrations when the need arises. Work with your technology support staff to decide how student work will be backed up—ideally, every day. Will students copy their work to floppy disks at the end of the day? Can you upload the whole project to a server each night? Every day without a backup means a day's work that can be lost.

FIGURE 5.3 SAMPLE FILING SYSTEM

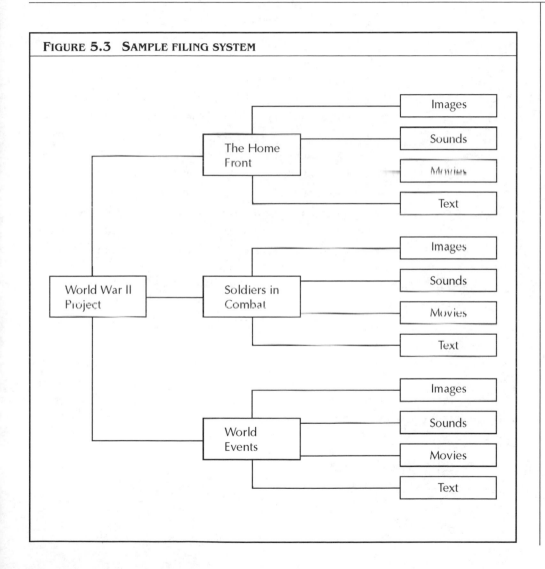

Prepare the Classroom

Organize books, computer manuals, printer paper, and any other resources so students can access them independently. Make room on the bulletin boards for hanging printouts of student work, schedules, and organizational charts.

Pay attention to the physical arrangement of technology tools. Place computers near each other in your classroom, if at all possible. So much independent learning occurs as students sit near each other and explore computer software. They share advice and learning tips on an as-needed basis. This frees you from having to respond to each question and distributes expertise in a natural way. If peripheral tools like scanners or movie production devices are in short supply, then you may want to save one computer for specialized use. Doing so will allow you to give special maintenance attention to the computer that scans and digitizes.

Finally, if you are new to multimedia production, don't have more than three to five computers running at one time. More than that is impossible to manage without a well-trained student assistant or a technology teacher at your side. By knowing the educational outcomes in advance, you can manage your classroom with a mix of technology and nontechnology activities so that you reduce the number of computers in use.

Introducing the Project
(One or Two Days)

In the first days of your project, you will probably be working to help students develop a "big picture" understanding of the work ahead. They should understand what they will be making, who their audience is, and what you expect them to learn and demonstrate in terms of the curriculum. The 15-minute video *Multimedia: A Sneak Preview,* available on line from WestEd at http://www.wested.org/cs/wew/view/rs/609, can help you introduce your project. The following activities can help as you develop ideas to do this.

Review Project Documents

You can ask students to work with the project documents you have produced. They can create a large display of the schedule you can all use to check progress, or they can write questions for a preassessment based on your learning goals. This gives them an opportunity to ask questions about the project to clarify what you have written.

Perform Pre-assessments

See Chapter 6 for ideas for pre-assessments that also help develop the big picture for students.

Perform Relevant Activities

You can show students anything you can find that is similar to what they will be producing, such as a similar offline paper and pencil project your students did last year, a Web site, or your own miniproject you did to learn the technology. You can also brainstorm for topics, organizational ideas, and design ideas.

Primary source documents can strengthen the real-world connection at this stage. A teacher started a math project on architecture by bringing in the blueprints for her own house. Students were fascinated by the peek into her house and worked hard to understand the scale drawings on the blueprints.

Group Students

Now is the time to form small student groups. Most of the teachers we work with prefer to form groups of three to five students. If students will have a large role in deciding the subject matter and organization of the project, you may want to form the groups *after* the preliminary research and concept design phase so students can group themselves according to the organization of the project. Here are some grouping strategies:

A technology learning coordinator organized project teams according to the perspectives of different scientific disciplines. She explains, "For our last multimedia product students created presentations to demonstrate one aspect of water pollution. The project teams each took a different dimension. We had chemists, physicists, botanists, zoologists, artists and writers, meteorologists, geographers, and historians."

- ***By topic interest.*** For projects that have well-defined subtopics, students can select a first and second choice, and you can form roughly equal groups based on their choices.
- ***By student talent and expertise.*** Explain that multimedia requires many different kinds of talents and skills. Ask students to rate their top skills in subjects like writing, researching, drawing, using technology, and organizing information. Create groups so talents and skills are balanced.
- ***By student choice.*** Ask each student to name two people they want to work with, and try to give everyone at least one of their choices. That way no student is completely left out of a group.
- ***Randomly.*** This is fine—part of project-based learning is to develop the skills to work with others, even by the luck of the draw.

Organize Materials

Give each group a folder that stays in the classroom. All their group work, such as storyboards, group journals, and research notes, goes in that folder so that the group isn't brought to a halt when one member is absent.

Learning the Technology (One to Three Days)

At this stage of the project, students certainly don't need to learn every facet of the authoring tool they will be working with. The goal here is to add to their understanding of the big picture by giving them a chance to work (or play) with whatever software and technology they will be using. Thus, as they plan they will have a better sense of what ideas are realistic and how long things take.

If some students are already familiar with the tools and processes, you are in luck—you can ask them to help you train the others. If not, you can create a few experts in one after-school session.

Give your students a simple, well-defined task to do, in groups or individually, that leads them through the basics of creating, for example, a Web page or a PowerPoint slide. Let them photograph themselves with the digital camera and put their picture on a Web page, or scan a picture from a magazine and import it. The task can be goofy and fun, but it should be simple and easy.

If students are new to multimedia, then begin with lessons that involve using the different media types. For instance, if you are studying about nature, you may want to spend a class making digital images about your environment. Or you may want to collect the sounds around you. Practicing with one media type at a time can give you a sense of how to manage resources and time before you embark on a full-fledged multimedia production.

Remember, you and your students will have to learn as you go. *Teacher as colearner* is a new relationship for many people. Waiting until you know it all is impossible when it comes to multimedia. Remember that you can't do it all; asking for help is okay, even if it's from your students.

You will find that you and your students continue to learn new features and processes as you use the technology throughout the project. An elementary school teacher taught short lessons as new features were discovered or needed. She explains, "Whenever I wanted to demonstrate something new on the computer, I called the children over to the Computer Alley. They sat on the floor or stood to see what I was doing on the computer. This was the way I introduced a number of activities related to PowerPoint and Kid Pix Studio. This is where my student helpers came in handy. I could count on them to learn quickly and help others."

The first year I did this project, computer access was so limited that I arranged a one-day field trip to a facility with all the computers, memory, software, and so forth that I needed. I spent that day teaching my students Adobe Photoshop and Adobe Premiere and they got their projects started.

—MIDDLE SCHOOL TEACHER

Not all projects involve book research. A 4th and 5th grade class planned a multimedia project based on artist Hokusai's *36 Views of Mount Fuji*. Each student created a drawing, photograph, and haiku based on his or her own view of a single object at the school. Research and planning involved touring the school grounds and searching for the perfect object. They settled on the play structure, because it was a good size, had interesting shapes, and looked different from different directions.

Preliminary Research and Planning (Three Days to Three Weeks, Depending on Project Size)

At this stage, students should immerse themselves in the content or subject matter they need to understand to create their presentations. Students will engage in relevant experiences or conduct research to collect information and gather ideas. Field trips, teacher-guided lessons, student research, interviews, observation, and questioning are all activities that might occur during this stage.

Students can tag and collect information they think might be valuable for their presentations: compelling photographs, quotes, sounds, and other media they encounter in their research. During field trips, they can take photographs for their presentations. Students can keep records of URLs (uniform resource locators or Web addresses) and content of Web sites they find. This is a good time to emphasize fair-use and plagiarism issues, as well as the importance of crediting sources.

Concept Design and Storyboarding (Three to Five Days)

After collecting initial information, hold a brainstorming session where the whole class or a subgroup defines a tentative approach to the subject and discusses some preliminary design ideas. Now that students know something about the subject matter, what do they want to say? How best can they address their client's or audience's needs and interests? What is the primary message, and how will they organize their information to present it?

Now is the time to talk about organizing a presentation to make it useful to the audience. Your students probably have quite a bit of experience with how Web sites are usually organized and can tell stories of interfaces that caused difficulties.

As a class or in groups, sketch out your overall design for the presentation. Then have groups create their *storyboards*.

A storyboard is a paper-and-pencil sketch of the entire presentation, screen by screen or, in the case of video, shot by shot. Each pane of the storyboard shows what text, images, sounds, motion, and interactivity buttons will go on the screen and how they will be arranged. There should be no beautiful drawings or full color (unless it's necessary to show a point of design). This is a quick sketch; time spent making it beautiful is time wasted. The panes are connected with lines to show how the presentation flows. For example, a home page with six buttons for six topics connects to six topic screens from each button.

Requiring a storyboard provides a natural check-in point for you and gives your students an opportunity to plan ahead. Then, when other questions arise, the flow chart or storyboard becomes a concrete reference point for what to do next.

Here are a few design tips to keep in mind throughout storyboarding and production:

• Use scanned, handmade artwork to make a project look personal and to manage scarce technology resources. Student artwork is unmatched as a way to assure a project has heart. Keep clip art or stamps to a minimum—they make a presentation look canned.

• Keep navigation—the way users of your presentation will get from one screen to the next—consistent throughout the whole presentation. "Back" and "Next" buttons, if you have them, should appear at the same place on

Content immersion can happen many places. One class took a photography field trip to the zoo in preparation for their presentation about animals of the rain forest. Later, they researched the animals at the library and on the Internet. Having taken their own photographs, they were doubly excited to find out more about "their" animals.

each screen (for example, the lower right corner). Always include a way to get to the home page or the beginning of the presentation.

• Organize information similarly throughout so users can find what they are looking for.

• Use colors and patterns to enhance the message. Students often sink a lot of time into making fancy backgrounds because the software allows them to and then end up with screens that are impossible to read.

• Use sounds to enhance the message as well. Those annoying transition sounds that come with presentation programs are almost sure to detract from your students' message.

First Draft Production (One to Three Weeks)

If you and your students are new to project-based multimedia, start with a preliminary production phase so that everyone gains experience in production before finalizing ideas about the overall design. Ask student groups to construct easy pieces of their presentation. They can create simple slide shows, or something similar, such as single Web pages that can be assembled into an overall piece with navigational choices or links. Develop any technological rules students need to follow so that the media elements will work together when assembled. Review and enforce your conventions for naming and organizing computer files.

After preliminary production might be a good time for a quick first assessment activity, such as a design review (see Chapter 6). Students can revise their initial design and concept—often the first ideas will prove too complicated to finish by the deadline.

Now you will be in full production of the first draft. The following tips can keep you focused and productive.

Avoid Loss of Work

• ***Save, save, save!*** Beginners often lose days of work because files haven't been saved properly or information is not backed up. Use a kitchen timer if necessary to get students into the habit of saving frequently—when the buzzer sounds, everyone saves. How often should students save their work? That is like asking, "How much work are you willing to lose if the computer crashes?" Students should save work every 5 to 10 minutes and after any complex or difficult operation.

• ***Back up.*** Establish a daily routine for backing up all student files (that is, making a second copy somewhere else—on a disk, zip drive, or another computer). Students can do this themselves as part of their end-of-day wrap-up.

Care for Equipment

Many of the following procedures are simple enough that they can be assigned to students or parent helpers, so don't feel you have to do it all yourself.

• ***Arrange for regular maintenance of computers.*** Running multimedia software is hard on your computer's operating system. A regularly scheduled, weekly maintenance routine will eliminate many problems before they begin. Most PCs have built-in system utilities (small programs) that you can run to check the health, or working order, of your computer. Because each brand is slightly different, you should ask your computer technology specialist or the local computer dealer how to locate this utility on your PC. If you are using a Mac, you will need to purchase something like Norton Utilities. Running this program at least once per week will save a lot of difficulties later.

• ***Develop procedures for maintaining and caring for peripherals.*** Difficulties with ancillary equipment such as cameras and tape recorders come most frequently when batteries are not charged in advance. To get into the habit of charging batteries, keep a sign on the wall near the equipment to remind you. Lost pieces are the second most frequent problem in schools. As soon as you receive cameras and so forth, purchase a carrying bag and prepare a list of contents. Then, devise a check-out/check-in system to account for the parts after every use. If you have the funds, purchase a hard carrying case rather than a soft one. For some reason, students take better care of equipment that is stored in more professional-looking cases.

• ***Keep everything clean.*** Refer to equipment manuals for how to clean camera lenses, video heads, keyboards, and other surfaces that collect dirt.

• ***Limit solo troubleshooting.*** Sometimes an error results from software or hardware troubles beyond your control. Don't always assume that you are the one at fault. The safest way to avoid spending endless hours troubleshooting is to set a time limit. Say to yourself, "I will work on this problem for up to 30 minutes, and then I will ask for help." Besides the obvious sources of help, like your computer-savvy friend or the school technology specialist, you can access online technical support Web pages for most products. Look in your computer manuals or software guides for specific web addresses.

Help Students Work Efficiently

• *Ask students to prepare the media elements outside of the authoring program whenever possible.* Authoring programs are built to be containers for information created elsewhere. So, create the text elements in a word processing program and be sure to spell check. Then the text is ready to import or copy and paste into the authoring software. The same applies to graphics and sound. Create and optimize the files before importing them.

• *Enforce considerate use of equipment.* Here is a scene you want to avoid: A student stands at the scanner leafing through a pile of books looking for pictures as the line of frustrated students grows longer behind her. Make sure students are as prepared as they can be before they get a turn with equipment.

• *Keep the technology simple relative to students' skill level.* Often the focus on learning gets diverted from a specific topic and learning technology becomes the focus instead. This shift leads many teachers to feel dissatisfied with the experience. To avoid getting lost in the technology learning, keep the multimedia simple. Ask students about their topics with questions like, "How does that image choice relate to what you are trying to say about (your topic)?" If you stay relentlessly focused on learning goals, your students will too.

Too much "technology talk" is a sign that you may need to limit the *tool set.* That is, the technology has become too complicated or is too engrossing to serve as a tool. You can insist that students use only certain tools or that they have to have content in place and approved before they can spend time adding flashiness to their presentations.

Students who appear to be focusing on technology may in fact be learning important curriculum-related skills. In one project, two high school students interviewed an older man. In the course of the interview the man told many captivating stories, but each story shifted to another and then reverted back to the original. The students had to listen to the entire interview, select portions that would serve as a beginning, middle, and end, and then learn how to integrate these sound bites into an audio file that flowed as though it were the original telling. After logging the tape at home, they spent two 90-minute class periods putting the segments together. By going through this time-consuming routine, they learned some new technology. But more importantly, they learned the organization of thought, learned details from the historical period, and attended to language syntax and inflection as they sought to create a fluid story.

Efficiency improves as you and your students become more expert with a piece of software. For example, HyperStudio allows two easy ways to put text in a presentation. One teacher found out after design reviews that only one of the methods allows easy *revision* of the text. Unfortunately, her students had all used the other one! They were painfully and slowly reconstructing entire screens just to fix one typo. If you are new to a piece of software, try to find a more experienced teacher to clue you in to pitfalls like this.

• ***Care for collaboration.*** Check in with groups to make sure they are collaborating successfully and that conflict is not derailing their productivity. Chapter 6 contains suggestions for assessing collaboration. As you observe groups working well, share stories of good collaboration with the rest of the class. Use group journals or logs to make sure everyone is contributing. Offer to facilitate problem-solving sessions with groups that are having trouble. Break up a group that seems really hopeless. Offer strategies to minimize the impact of an unproductive student on the group product.

• ***Organize manageable steps.*** School schedules and the time that project-based multimedia learning requires often come into conflict. Forty-five minute class times are short and must involve an incredible amount of organization if your project is to be successful. Therefore, it is important to break down the project's steps into manageable daily components.

• ***Check and assess often.*** A mistake caught at the storyboard stage is easy to fix. A mistake in the final product is often impossible to fix.

• ***Be ready to redirect.*** What will you do if a severe electrical storm destroys all your computers? This is when you find out if all the work you've done was valuable in itself, or if it depended completely on the computers. With a good project design, your students have been learning all along. You simply redefine what the product will be. For example, you may decide to take the source materials and film a video of students explaining or presenting them. It's not what you hoped for, but the students achieved your curriculum goals, and that is what is most important.

Assessing, Testing, and Finalizing Presentations (One to Three Weeks)

It's time to start testing and assessing when groups have their presentations limping along with most elements integrated. Notice this stage's duration— we have allowed about a third of the project time for it because so much significant learning happens here.

There are two kinds of testing to think about: functional testing and user testing. Functional testing means trying all the buttons, taking all possible paths through the presentation, checking for errors, missing images, and the like. User testing means showing the presentation to members of the target audience and finding out if they can successfully navigate it and understand it. For example, if your target audience is younger students, user testing would include watching those students go through the presentation and making sure the text is appropriate for their reading level.

Assessment means critical evaluation of your presentation. Ideally this comes from more than one source. Possible assessors include your students, you, members of your target audience, content experts, and design experts. Chapter 6 explores assessment more fully and contains assessment activities that can be used at various stages of the project.

The key idea about testing and assessing is this: You *have* to do it while students still have time to fix the problems they find, or students will find the enterprise pointless and demoralizing. And they will be right.

After assessment and testing, your students will be revising and making a "release candidate," a version everyone thinks is just about perfect. The release candidate is tested further, and at this stage no new content or features are added. Only things like crashes, mortifying factual errors or offensive material, and typos are fixed. After a round of fixes, you make a new release candidate and test it. This process continues until the deadline. *If you're out of time, you're out of time, so stop!* The last release candidate becomes the final version, which you post, copy, archive, or deliver as appropriate. If there are serious problems with the final version and you have a client or real-world audience, just add a "read me" file or page that warns the user about these problems and (if you know) explains how they might be fixed.

Concluding Activities (One to Three Days)

Allow time for students to present and show off their hard work. You and they will be proud of what they have done and will want to share it with others. Concluding activities make a memorable project even more special.

Often there is an obvious, authentic concluding activity related to your real-world connection. You will present to your target audience and celebrate your accomplishment. You can also think about scheduling your project so the end coincides with a school event, such as Parents' Night or a year-end party. You can organize an exhibition day with other teachers where the school views all the multimedia projects for the semester. (See Chapter 9 for more about multimedia fairs.) You might also consider submitting the project to a multimedia competition.

Remember to take time to review the ups and downs of the project with students and anyone else who participated. Take notes on suggestions for things to do differently next year.

One middle school teacher worked with other teachers and technology experts to decide how to improve infrastructure for next year. She reports that they came up with several good ideas: "We made a few changes that should make technology use easier. We put a better security system on the computers at the end of the year to help with the deliberate breaking down of equipment. We also added some memory. Multimedia takes tons."

6

The Roles of Assessment

Assessment is such a big topic. Perhaps you come to this chapter wondering how you'll know what students have learned. Or maybe you are looking for a good rubric to use or, at least, advice on how to create your own. Maybe you want to keep tabs on student learning throughout the project. Perhaps you are looking for ways to involve students in the assessment process. Because you are doing something new, you may also be interested in how you can document student learning for outside audiences like your principal, other teachers, or parents—particularly if they are skeptical about whether making multimedia projects is a good use of your students' time.

Project-based multimedia learning is different from direct teaching in many ways. One key way is that students diverge from one another a great deal more. In fact, adding the multimedia component to project-based learning seems to accelerate this divergence. Every work group has different goals, work styles, creative energy, and relevant skill sets. Before you know it, students will be heading down different paths from one another; some paths will address your curricular goals and some may not. Assessment is your best hope for keeping everyone focused, maintaining a common baseline of learning, and ending up with a product you all will be proud of.

Three Areas of Assessment

We can break up our approach to assessment into manageable pieces by focusing on three areas that require constant attention throughout a multimedia project.

 • *Area 1. Assessment activities for developing expectations and standards.* This means working with your students to define what constitutes evidence of learning and what constitutes a high-quality multimedia project. This area requires focused attention at the beginning of a project and then refinement throughout. Attending to expectations and standards will give you a common reference for focusing and make it easier for everyone to stay on track.

 • *Area 2. Assessment activities for catalyzing project improvement and learning.* As students work, you and they can periodically assess their work in relation to your expectations and standards. These assessments give students concrete direction for improving their work and deepening their learning.

 • *Area 3. Assessment activities for compiling and disseminating evidence of student learning.* Throughout the project, you and your students collect evidence of learning and meeting standards. Toward the end of the project you can organize this information into forms suitable for outside audiences, such as grades.

In short, the three areas are

1. Defining what "good" is.
2. Making the project good.
3. Describing how well it turned out.

This may sound like a step-by-step process, but it rarely works out that way. To understand this, imagine you hire a painter to paint your kitchen. You tell the painter you want a nice cheery yellow, but not too bright. These are your initial standards. You and the painter look at paint chips together, trying to clarify your standards. What does a "nice cheery yellow" mean to you? You choose a color and the painter begins to work. After working for a while, the painter calls you in to take a look (make an assessment). You realize that the color that looked right on a chip is actually too pale (you continue to clarify your standards in terms of what you see). You also notice that the painter has accidentally gotten paint on the cabinets, and you ask her to be more careful (you make an implicit standard more explicit). You see how this one area—deciding what good is—is an ongoing process, or at least it should be if you want your kitchen to turn out well. It's the same with multimedia. You could hand students the most detailed standards in the world and you would still need to help them relate the words in the standards to the multimedia on the screen. What does it mean for multimedia to be "clear," "visually interesting," or "well-organized"? Students come to understand these terms only when they are related to real work. Attending to standards in real time also helps you account for stylistic differences between students and classes year after year, since each new group has a chance to be involved in the process of negotiating standards and exemplars.

Luckily, the three areas, though ongoing, often can be addressed with assessment techniques that overlap two or three areas. That is, one assessment may both help define "good" and help students improve their projects. So it's not as hard as it may sound.

Using Assessment Activities to Address the Three Areas

Now let's take a look at some typical assessment activities and discuss how you can use them to address our three areas. We'll look at three activities: one typically thought of as being about defining "good," one typically about making projects better, and one about telling how good it is. We'll see how each activity can be used to address multiple roles of assessment.

Activity 1: Creating an Assessment Document

You are probably going to need a document such as a checklist (a list of terms that describe a high-quality project) or a rubric (a grid describing several levels of quality). Your document will serve as a reference point for all assessments. It should not be set in stone—you will probably want to revise it as you progress. At a minimum, it should embody your project requirements and learning goals.

For example, suppose you are a 3rd grade teacher doing a language arts project where students create multimedia versions of original stories. Your curriculum goals, translated into language kids understand, would become part of your checklist or rubric. The checklist in Figure 6.1, adapted from the California State Content Standards for 3rd grade, might be part of your checklist for your students. You can develop such a checklist as a way to start describing to your students what you mean by a good project (Area 1).

FIGURE 6.1 AN ASSESSMENT CHECKLIST	Yes	No
Does your story have details?		
Do your characters use actions to show what they are like?		
Do the pictures help us understand the story?		
Can others understand what happens in your story?		
Does your story use complete sentences?		
Are all words spelled correctly?		

Suppose, though, you want to use the process of developing a checklist to encourage and support students in improving their stories (Area 2). In that case, you will certainly want to involve students in the development of the checklist. You might show them some existing multimedia storybooks and ask what they like about them. One student might say, "I like the big heavy boots the bad guy wears." You say, "Oh, do those boots help you see he's a bad guy? So you think a good story uses details like clothes to tell us about

My 2nd graders could not wait to get started after seeing last year's slide presentation of the whale watching trip made with Kid Pix Studio. They made suggestions on how we could make this year's better. When I asked them what they thought a good presentation should include they easily volunteered the following: beginning, middle, and end, descriptive words, important facts and events, feelings about the trip, pictures, and proper spelling. I posted their ideas on a chart for future reference. They also expressed that their writing should be sequential and make sense. During the days that followed as the aide, student teacher, and I met with the pairs for conferencing we were able to hold them accountable for the criteria that they set for themselves.

—ELEMENTARY TEACHER

The longer the project, the more the students are likely to feel they own it. And consequently, the more they should be allowed a voice in the assessment.

—HIGH SCHOOL TEACHER

characters?" At the end of the discussion, you have a list of project characteristics generated by the students themselves. You can almost guarantee that the child who pointed out the boots will have a detail like that in his story, and so will several other children. Your finished list will include your curricular goals but also some things the students came up with that are important to them.

What about Area 3? If you are thinking ahead to the task of grading projects, creating an exhibition for an outside audience, or some other culminating assessment, you might work your requirements into the design of the rubric or checklist. For example, suppose you want to use your checklist to show how doing a multimedia project helped your students meet district writing standards. Will you be able to do that, or do you need a second document written expressly for that purpose? You may end up making a special version of your assessment document that serves your own accountability requirements.

Activity 2: Whole-Class Design Review

In a whole-class design review, students present work in progress to the class for feedback. The work in progress might be a storyboard, a partly implemented piece of multimedia, or any of the building blocks the project requires. The idea behind using work in progress is that students are more willing to take suggestions and make improvements when input comes before the end. As one student remarked, "I like getting suggestions in the middle of creating something. At the end, I just want people to enjoy my work. I don't want to hear anything more about what I could have done."

Whether the work you choose for critique is a planning tool, like a storyboard, or the actual production itself, using well-defined rules and procedures for looking at student work will create a safer environment for students who present. The basic rules for safety in discussion center on two elements: first, making direct observations rather than rushing to scoring judgments, and second, paying attention to what the production group is trying to do. For examples of protocols for looking at student work and more specific explanation of critiquing work in progress, visit The WEB Project (http://www.webproject.org) or the Looking at Student Work consortium (http://www.lasw.org).

Because you are using your previously developed assessment document, it may sound strange to say that a whole-class design review helps define what "good" is. It is actually one of the best things you can do for that purpose, provided you and your students use specific and detailed comments that speak to what the production team is trying to do.

For example, you can use the checklist in Figure 6.1 for a multimedia storybook project. One item is "Does your story have details?" A whole-class design review is one good way to elaborate on such an item. In the discussions, it might become clear that one can have too many or too few details, that the details can aid or distract the reader, or that the details can be appropriate or inappropriate for the character or setting. Students can emerge with a much more sophisticated understanding of the level of quality implied by the checklist item. In other words, a good story has details, and the details should be helpful and appropriate. You might even add these things to your assessment document to help students remember what they have figured out. What about catalyzing project improvements? A whole-class design review shines in this area, and not just because of the feedback students receive. Students are often surprised and delighted by creative ideas they see in other groups' projects, and every good idea tends to raise the bar for the whole class. Similarly, when students observe suggestions for improvement in other projects that apply to theirs as well, they will eagerly make their changes without even waiting for the design review. For students who are having trouble figuring out how to do the project at all, seeing the other groups' work in progress makes the task much clearer. We have found in our research that students are much more likely to revise their projects after a whole-class design review and that nearly every revision can be directly traced to something that came up in the review. Your review will be particularly effective if you help students record issues and suggestions that arise and ask them to respond in writing. Ask them to detail which comments will be helpful in improving their work and how they will implement these ideas.

Student-written responses can become data they will use later as evidence of learning (Area 3). At the end of the project, students can write a reflection using these and other artifacts they created as points in the story of their learning. They can describe how each stage helped them see new questions and deepened their understanding.

Activity 3: Content Assessments

Here is an annoying thing about multimedia projects, particularly collaborative group projects: it is difficult to tell what students know just by assessing their multimedia projects. This is not just because you don't know who did all the work but because students have to learn more than might be evident in their final products. Making good multimedia is a process of sifting through a lot of information and including only the most compelling.

If you are responsible for covering a content-rich curriculum, you will probably want to assess students' content learning in some way other than looking at their project. There are many ways to do this, from a traditional test to a written reflection to an oral interview. You can do it at the end of the research phase, at the end of the project, or both.

A content assessment done midway through the project is good for helping to define good content and for encouraging students to be more rigorous in exploring it. It is actually a good idea to assess students' content knowledge before they get too far into multimedia. Otherwise students can put a lot of effort into making multimedia out of inaccurate content, only to have to redo it later. On the other hand, keep in mind that students will deepen their content understanding as they create their presentations.

A content assessment excels, of course, in letting everyone know how much your students have learned as they worked on their multimedia projects. In fact, one teacher we know gave a content assessment after teaching a unit on a biology topic but before doing the multimedia project. Her students did well on all of it except the part that required thinking and extrapolation about the topic. Students then completed a multimedia project that involved computer modeling of the biological phenomena. After the multimedia project, she gave the same assessment again, and now her students were able to think beyond the facts and reason with the material. She was able to see that the multimedia project was responsible for moving her students past the simple recall level to a deeper understanding of the topic. This sort of pre/post-testing can be extremely useful in demonstrating your students' growth in knowledge and understanding.

Creating an Assessment Plan

Assessment is to learning as coffee is to energy—it can energize and focus effort. Every time you ask students to participate in the critical examination of their work, they are going to learn something just by participating in the assessment and then become energized to work harder. Deciding where you need to put assessment activities in your project is a matter of deciding when students will probably need that boost to propel them into the next stage. To continue with the analogy, too much coffee can make you a trembling wreck, and so it is with too much assessment. Finding that balance between doing and reflecting is the art of making an assessment plan.

To begin your assessment, think of a matrix like the one in Figure 6.2 and fill it with assessment activities—one or two in each cell. Remember that some activities will appear in more than one cell because they advance more than one instructional goal or take on more than one assessment role.

FIGURE 6.2 AN ASSESSMENT PLANNING MATRIX			
	Instructional Goal 1	Instructional Goal 2	Instructional Goal 3
Area 1. Defining "good"			
Area 2. Making projects good			
Area 3. Describing how well they turned out			

Figure 6.3 (pp. 94–97) shows a generic project with notes about various assessment activities. We've marked each assessment activity as being particularly strong in one or more of our three areas. You can adapt the ideas to your project, aiming for a series of assessments that gives you a balance across the three areas. A good way to begin is to make a list of your two or three most important instructional goals for the project, and focus all your assessments on those.

Keep in mind that assessment, although it's incredibly valuable, does add to everyone's workload. You will probably want to keep your plan simple, particularly at first. Include no more than one or two formal activities at each stage of your project, and perhaps leave some stages with no formal assessment. As long as you do some checking in with your students as they work, you can probably keep things on track for some time.

The suggestions in this chapter should get you started. Don't forget your most tried and true assessment practices—most can be adapted to a multimedia project.

When I talk with students during class, I can do in 30 minutes in groups of 5 or 6 what would take me longer with homework. I can say, "OK, is this every shot? Who's getting the audio? This revision—is it any good? Have you addressed concerns? That's an A then." I just make a check.

—HIGH SCHOOL TEACHER

FIGURE 6.3 ASSESSMENT ACTIVITIES

Possible Assessment Activities
1 = Defining what "good" is.
2 = Making the project good.
3 = Describing how well it turned out.

Pre-assessment (3): Find out what students already know about the topic through a pretest, a discussion, an essay, or whatever works. That helps students begin focusing and thinking about the topic and generates baseline data to compare with the final assessment.

Storyboard pre-assessment (2, 3): Ask students to make a quick storyboard as if they are making the presentation today, using what they already know about their project topic. You can compare this to the final project and measure student growth.

Peer assessment of technology skills (2, 3): Make a list of tasks you want every student to be able to do with the software. Have students check off their group members on each skill. Spot check if you want. That way, no matter who is absent, someone in the group can run the software.

Journals (2, 3): You can start journals here. Students, individually or as a group, write entries about what they are having trouble finding, what they have found useful, etc. You respond with suggestions, pointing them to resources or other students who can help them.

Assess notes (1, 2): You can also provide written feedback on students' research notes.

Walkaround (2): This is the most important assessment activity. Walk around as students work, talk to them about what they are doing, ask them hard questions about the content, take time to explain a sticky point.

FIGURE 6.3   ASSESSMENT ACTIVITIES—*continued*

Making an assessment document (1, 2, 3): For example, a rubric or checklist. This is a good time to do it because students have some idea about content and design.

Component check-off (3): You might check that all the necessary components have been finished, especially for younger students. For example, photographs chosen and scanned, drawings scanned, research notes complete, etc.

More journals (1, 2, 3): Ask students to note what information or other resources they need for their presentations. Ask them to record their process. How are they deciding what information to use? What have they decided to leave out of their presentation? What parts of their storyboards exemplify terms from your rubric or checklist?

Use your assessment document to assess storyboards (1, 2, 3): Students can get some practice using your criteria. This can be done as an individual written reflection, a peer review, or a teacher-student conference. The important thing is not to give the storyboard a rubric rating but to say what aspects of the storyboard match the criteria in the rubric. "My presentation will be clear," a student might write, "because I have illustrations that accompany each text description."

Mid-project content assessment (2, 3): This is a good time to assess students' understanding of subject matter content before they begin working with technology. Your assessment might be a performance assessment, a test, an essay, or an oral interview.

Walkaround (2): Talk with students about what you see on their screens. Make sure they really understand the text they are writing. Ask them why they chose particular illustrations.

Collaboration assessments (1, 2, 3): There are many ways to assess collaboration. You can directly observe a group for 10 minutes or so, and check off the collaborative

FIGURE 6.3 ASSESSMENT ACTIVITIES—*continued*

behaviors you see. You can ask students to record what they did for their group each day. You can videotape short segments of group work and ask the class to comment on the helpful and hindering behaviors they see. You can ask each student to assess each member of his or her group on their collaboration.

Mid-project design review(s) (1, 2, 3): This can be the whole-class design review, a peer review, or a teacher-student conference. Work in progress can also be assessed by members of the target audience for your students' presentations or by outside subject matter or design experts.

Revisit your assessment document (1): As students become more sophisticated in their judgments, ask them what might need to be added or clarified.

More journals (1, 2): Ask students to continue to record their process. If you are assessing collaboration, you might ask groups to keep records of individual contributions and write to you if they need help getting their group to function productively. On some days, you might ask students to assess their projects in terms of one item on your rubric or checklist and provide justification for their assessments.

Walkaround (2): Make sure students have the resources they need to do the improvements they want to do.

Check-off of revisions (3): Ask students to report on the revisions they did and how their project has improved.

Final scoring with assessment document (3): Each project gets a final evaluation with your rubric or checklist.

FIGURE 6.3   ASSESSMENT ACTIVITIES—*continued*

Final exhibition or presentation (2, 3): Give students a chance to present their finished work to an outside audience—at best, to the target audience for which the presentation was developed. You'll be amazed how students scramble to perfect their work.

End of project content assessments (3): These are like the mid-project assessments, except they are given at the end.

Post-assessment that matches pre-assessment (3): If you did a pre-assessment at the beginning of the unit, give it again to measure students' growth.

Assigning a project grade (3): Most teachers do this by assigning points to various assessments along the way and to the final assessments. For example, students might get 5 points for the technology skill assessment; 10 points for each journal entry; 30 points for collaboration assessments; 30 points for the mid-project reflection after the design review; 30 points for the revision check-off; and 60 points each for the content assessment and the project scoring. Then students are assigned a grade based on the percentage of possible points they earned.

Sharing the good news (3): Organize your pre/post data for a presentation to other faculty, PTA, or administration. Include some of your students and their projects in the presentation.

7

Teachers and Students: Evolving Roles

What's your image of the stereotypical teacher? Do you see a conservatively dressed lady with her hair in a bun, a sharpened pencil tucked behind her ear, methodically writing the homework assignment on the chalkboard in perfect cursive? A troubled, charismatic provocateur like the English teacher in *Dead Poets Society* who urges his students to "seize the day"? Does your mind's eye conjure a vision of a modern-day *Our Miss Brooks* who puts kids—not to mention colleagues and bumbling administrators—in their place with a wisecrack and a gimlet-like sideways glance? Or do you picture a self-effacing, compassionate, gently prodding taskmaster like Mr. Holland? Does your image match one of these? Yes? No? Is it a blend, or is it quite different? Whatever you see when you think "teacher," we predict that the person in your imagination shares some key behaviors with the images described here. You probably picture someone who spends a lot of time on his feet (while students spend most of their time on their bottoms!). Your teacher likely spends a good percentage of the day anchored in the front of the room talking to the class. She may also move about the room to check in with students and monitor their work. Most significantly, whether stationary or ambulatory, the teacher knows more about what's being taught than the kids do—and the teacher calls the shots. It's in these final ways that project-based multimedia learning diverges most from traditional ideas about what teachers are and do.

What Your Role Will *Not* Be

Teachers who try project-based multimedia learning typically experience two unexpected and often discomfiting changes in their role. First, they are no longer the singular experts in their classrooms—particularly relating to technology. Even in the lower grades, kids often know more about computers and software programs than their teachers do. When they don't, they still learn faster than their teachers, so they quickly catch up and surpass them in their technological prowess. Although this may be unnerving, it is fairly easy to accept because, as subject matter experts, few of us have been required or expected to master a technology that is quickly becoming part of children's lives from an early age. Yet, at the same time, we're used to being better talkers, better readers, better writers, and better *you-name-its* than our students. It does cause us a bit of angst when even our learning-challenged students can use new tools better than we can.

But there is a more unsettling challenge with which project-based multimedia teachers must come to grips. During project work, students often delve deeply into a certain topic or aspect of a subject. As they do so, they may acquire more knowledge about the topic than their teacher has. For example,

Project-based multimedia learning has really changed my actual and perceived role in the classroom. I am still in charge but in a more dynamic way. I now make judgments about what concepts I will be teaching instead of letting the text make those decisions. I am no longer the sole font of wisdom, but I am still respected because my students know that if I do not know something, I will find a place for them to go to figure it out. Also, I respect that they have a lot of wisdom to give me so that we all learn from each other. This strategy allows all of us to become the best that we can be.
—MIDDLE SCHOOL TEACHER

It was after lunch. My class was in the computer lab working on a project called Dreamhouse, where the students were designing houses for imaginary clients. The students are all working, some in the middle of the room working on sketching designs, some at the computers drawing the designs, some sitting behind the computer operators telling them what they should or should not be doing. I had already checked with those still in the planning stages and they were fine, making progress on sketching their designs or creating needs lists. As I stood in the middle of the room, I felt at that moment that I was really unneeded. If I walked out of the classroom and went to the lounge, would anyone even know that I was not there?

—MIDDLE SCHOOL TEACHER

if students in a biology class form small teams and each team thoroughly studies a particular disease, its etiology, and its treatment, the students on the team would likely end up knowing more about the disease than their teacher does.

A shift in control is the second change faced by teachers who embrace the project-based multimedia approach. As you know by now, student decision making is one of the essential dimensions of this type of learning, so some of this change in control is by design. As teachers plan and construct their units, they try to think of all the important decisions that must be made as the project unfolds. Then they give careful thought to determining which of those decisions to reserve for themselves and which to turn over to the students. Teachers base this distribution on many factors, such as the nature of the subject matter; the relationship of the project to required standards and curriculum; and the age, maturity, and experience of their students. The bottom line is: teachers who use the project-based multimedia approach know that only by having the opportunity to make decisions can students learn to make good ones.

If this "premeditated" relinquishing of control were the only way in which teachers experienced the control shift, it would probably not cause much concern and might even go unnoticed. However, when a unit really takes off, there is a subtle and pervasive change in hegemony in the classroom. It's not that the students necessarily take over; it's the work that takes over. Often, students and teachers alike find that the demands of the project begin to dictate who does what, when they do it, how, and where. In fact, this can happen to such a degree that teachers sometimes feel unnecessary or unneeded.

Are you forming a troubling picture of a dispirited teacher who not only is clumsy with the technology but is faced with kids whose knowledge of various special topics may surpass her own? Is this a recipe for teacher burnout? Thankfully, it is not. Although the project-based multimedia approach can feel strange at first and is certainly a lot of work—especially in the early stages—only a few of the teachers we've worked with want to give it up once they've started. Despite the anxiety, self-doubt, lost files, and crashed computers, they find a sense of renewal; and they witness growth in their students that more than compensates for the hurdles that must be overcome.

What Your Role *Will* Be

So if you're not the expert and you're not the boss, what are you? It's become a cliché in school circles for many educators—especially those who give speeches at educational conferences—to talk about how teachers need to exchange the frumpy old role of "sage on the stage" for the new, modern role of "guide on the side." Some would even forsake the title "teacher" in favor of *learning facilitator*. It's true that with project-based multimedia, teachers guide and facilitate learning. But there is much more to the role than that. A few key metaphors can help provide a deeper understanding of how teachers we've worked with experience their role when they really get involved in this type of learning.

Our teachers often liken their role to that of *project manager*. As such, they have a host of responsibilities, not the least of which is planning. Many teachers find that the ultimate success of a project-based unit depends heavily on the thoroughness of advance planning. Once projects are underway, teachers provide coordination to ensure that things go according to plan. They meet with student groups to review progress and discuss the quality of completed components or subsections. They refer students experiencing

My role became more of a facilitator or project manager. While the students were writing, I observed that they needed help with descriptive words, so we had a mini lesson. We brainstormed words that describe whales and words that describe what whales do. Here was a real need and opportunity to use adjectives and descriptive phrases. Instead of saying, "I saw a whale dive into water," one student said, "I saw a huge whale dive into the deep ocean." A couple of students said, "I got it!" and quickly returned to their work.

—ELEMENTARY TEACHER

My entire teaching career, I had felt that I was in charge. I was the one who planned the lessons, decided how they would be presented, asked the questions, assigned the homework, chose the time for the tests and the items on the tests. Teaching was all about me, and if the students did not learn, it was because they were lazy or did not follow my directions or just were not paying attention to me.

My perceptions certainly have changed in the last few years. Now I realize that my real job is planning what needs to be learned and setting up situations where students can find the answers for themselves.

—MIDDLE SCHOOL TEACHER

difficulty to other students who have previously faced and overcome a similar problem. When they notice more than one group struggling with the same difficulty, they may convene the whole class for an impromptu brainstorming session. They broker conflicts over ideas, space, and equipment. They mediate squabbles among team members. They watch the clock, the calendar, and—if there is one—the budget.

Thinking of teaching as project management is helpful in understanding what it's like to be a project-based multimedia teacher, but it captures only part of the role. In their book *Approaches to Teaching* education professors Gary Fenstermacher and Jonas Soltis (1998) offer three additional metaphors, each of which helps us understand the complexity of the teacher's role. They are: the teacher as executive, the teacher as therapist, and the teacher as liberationist. Figure 7.1 highlights key types of behavior of each approach.

These three approaches contrast markedly. Purists would say they're mutually exclusive. Fenstermacher and Soltis agree, but they argue that even if, in theory, teachers can't be true to more than one of these roles at a time, teachers can and should combine them in practice:

> The normative nature of teaching demands a commitment to worthy educational values, and each of these three approaches contains something of value. If you are committed to having your students gain to the fullest extent possible from their experiences of schooling, we believe you must try to put these three approaches together somehow while avoiding the pitfalls of doing so. (p. 55)

FIGURE 7.1. FENSTERMACHER AND SOLTIS'S APPROACHES TO TEACHING

The Executive	**The Therapist**	**The Liberationist**
• Plans, implements, measures, revises. • Manages people and resources. • Makes decisions about what people will do, how they will do it, how long it will take, and standards for performance. • Ensures that students acquire predetermined and clearly specified knowledge and skills.	• Enables students to find meaning, gain self-knowledge, become authentic. • Attends to individual differences. • Is essentially a supporter and helper; avoids exerting unnecessary control. • Wants students to knowingly accept responsibility for the choices they make and their consequences.	• Emphasizes content, especially broad and deep conceptual understanding. • Sees moral and intellectual values as part of the content of teaching. • Believes that teachers must set the example for students, that students will learn as much from how their teachers teach as from the explicit content that is taught. • Avoids purely instrumental approaches; demands that work has value and purpose.

When teachers decide to take the plunge into the world of project-based multimedia learning, they are really taking on a risk. They are showing a willingness to play a role different from the traditional one they have been playing. They are willing to give up the time-honored role of being the expert in every thing. Most often they will find students who know much more about the technology than they do. Allowing students to be empowered is challenging at first, but many teachers find it rewarding and satisfying. These risk-taking teachers will still be navigating the ship but will often be put in the role of rolling up their shirt sleeves and becoming learners with their students.

—TECHNOLOGY LEARNING
COORDINATOR

In fact, our teachers do just that. They blend and juggle the roles of executive, therapist, and liberationist, assuming the role appropriate to the moment and the needs of the students and the situation.

Allowing the students to help design and create a multimedia project increased learning and productivity. They take more responsibility for applying, synthesizing, and developing new skills in order to successfully complete their projects and reinforce the concepts and data. I am free to roam the room and provide direct instruction when needed. I am more aware of where they are in the process at any given moment. These new roles bring about a new sense of accomplishment and pride that would not have otherwise existed. What more can I ask for?

—ELEMENTARY TEACHER

Teachers and Students as Partners

There's one more facet to the teacher's role in project-based multimedia learning that is essential to understand but for which it's hard to find a single metaphor. Perhaps *partner* captures it best. In many ways, teachers and students are partners in this type of enterprise. They're in the same boat. They share risks and profits, frustrations and successes. Figuratively, and often literally, teachers roll up their sleeves to work and learn alongside their students as colleagues.

Facilitating project-based learning, especially with multimedia, presents a lot of conflicts for a content area teacher. If the class is history, then the point is to learn more about history and to acquire some additional technology skills in the process. I remember working with a group that was learning about World War II. The project was to last for one week, using a double block of 90 minutes per day. In preparation, students read a lot about events leading up to the war and listened to some local oral history tapes that had been prepared by a previous year's class. We spent the first two days sharing information and planning the project design. On day three, a student unexpectedly brought in his grandfather. The man began talking in a deep and serious tone with the opening phrase, "Today is a very important day for you are about to learn what it was like to have been a prisoner of war." Suddenly, we all knew that nothing could be more important than listening to what he had to say.

He spoke wonderfully but did not complete his thoughts sequentially. A small group decided to place his narration on top of an animated map of his travels across Europe. Because the grandfather did not finish his thoughts, they needed to use Adobe Premiere to cut and paste a story. The students showed a real understanding of storytelling and language. They stitched together the right sequence of words to convey the grandfather's tale and manipulated the sound of his voice to simulate the correct rise and fall of his pitch. As they constructed the audio track, they exchanged headphones to critique their work, asking questions like, "Does it flow yet?"

My careful observation of student learning meant that I could no longer be the manager and teacher. This shift occurred "in the moment" rather than from a wise act of preplanning. However, what I noticed was that when I stopped being the person "in charge of the software," those who had just learned from me took charge. At this point, students were seeking information from each other based on needed expertise. I could step back and examine the overall direction and tone.

During this project, I stepped in and out of many roles. What I discovered is that there is a general pattern of movement from high structure and teacher-directed activities to shared determination to autonomy. However, this is not a lock-step process. Knowing about the existence of multiple roles leads to a stronger set of facilitation skills, each to be used as the moment requires.

—HIGH SCHOOL TEACHER

Certainly, the role of the teacher in project-based multimedia learning is a multifaceted one. Coach, wise counselor, producer, project manager, therapist, executive, liberationist, conversationalist, senior partner—there are many hats to shuffle and not much opportunity to get bored. Trying this type of learning for the first time will probably move you a bit out of your comfort zone—but then don't we expect that of our students every day? And if your experience is anything like that of the teachers who spoke to you in this chapter, your challenge to yourself will pay off in enhanced student learning and your own satisfaction as a teacher.

8

Finding Support for Your Project

I f you've read this far, you may perhaps be ready to dive in. Or perhaps you are like the Cowardly Lion in *The Wizard of Oz*, who asked only one thing of his pals: "Talk me out of it!"

If this is true, your next step is to look around for help and support that will get you through your project in one sane piece. Many kinds of help are available; finding and organizing support can be a project in itself. As with everything else in this book, the best advice is to start small and simple, using the resources closest to you first and adding resources as you need them and as you find them.

Realize that getting support *shouldn't* be your job alone. You may have to wait a little until your school district understands this, and find your own help in the meantime. That is why this subject is divided into two chapters. This chapter is for you, the teacher, trying to drum up enough support by yourself to successfully complete a project-based multimedia learning project. The next chapter is for anyone who wants to begin the process of *systemic* change through capacity-building strategies in a school or district.

Thinking Through Your Requirements

Because many kinds of support are needed, your first task is to think through your own support requirements. Are you a technology beginner? Do you need just a little technical help? Maybe you have instructional issues to work out. Maybe you would be fine if it weren't for your school's regressive culture. The following sections address different support issues and suggest ways to find appropriate help.

Help, I'm Scared of Mice (Computer Mice, That Is)!

You've often looked a little longingly (or maybe a little guiltily) at the computer lab. "This summer," you promise yourself, "I'll learn to use those computers." Meanwhile, it seems that everyone else is charging ahead, and you're afraid to ask for help.

First, look into ways to get comfortable with computers. The most direct way is to take a beginner's class, offered at many adult education schools, community centers, and community colleges. There, in the company of other beginners, an experienced computer user can answer all your questions. Many school districts also offer introductory training.

Another way to get started is to think of one small thing that you would like to do on a computer and get a friend or relative to show you how. Here are some ideas for small, "getting started" projects:

Before I started, it looked enormously complicated, overwhelmingly complicated. How were six kids going to work with one computer—didn't they all need their own? I didn't know how to deal with equipment. I look in other teachers' doors and it's chaos! I thought, I'm not going there!

—ELEMENTARY TEACHER

- Use the Internet to find a specific piece of information—airfares, a lesson plan, or information related to your favorite hobby.
- Write a business letter.
- Play a computer game.
- Talk with someone in an Internet "chat" room.
- Get an e-mail account and send someone an e-mail.

Most experienced computer users can do all these things, so don't hesitate to ask.

If you can find someone to show you how to turn on the computer and get to the Internet, you can take all sorts of beginners' courses and get simple how-to information at *Connected University* (http://cu.classroom.com).

I Need Equipment or Software

You will find it invaluable to do an inventory of your school's equipment and software. The school may have more than you thought. Find and write down the following information:

- **Computer model.** For example, Power Macintosh G3, Dell Inspiron 3000.
- **Memory.** For example, 64 megabytes. Most software requires a certain minimum amount of memory to run.
- **Hard disk size and available space.** For example, 1 gigabyte, 200 megabytes. Some software takes up a lot of space, and multimedia files also tend to be quite large. Information about the hard disk size can tell you if the computer is adequate.

- **Operating systems.** For example, Windows 2000, Mac OS 9.1. You need to know this when buying software because some software will only run on certain operating systems.
- **Software versions.** Find the version number of any multimedia software. This information will be especially helpful if you have to call the company to get technical support.
- **Network environment.** Are the computers you will use connected to a local network? If so, what are the rules or policies for using the network?

You'll need money or donations if the following apply:

- Your computers are too old, too slow, or have too little memory or hard disk space to run multimedia software.
- You have too few computers. It is possible to do a class project on one computer, but you really have to scale back.
- Multimedia software is nonexistent or is so old that it will be frustrating to use and hard to find support for. You can look on the manufacturer's Web site and compare the current version with the version you have. If they are selling version 9.1 and you have version 2.0, you probably need to upgrade.
- You don't have the peripherals you need for the project, such as a scanner or camera.

If it turns out you need equipment or software, here are some ways to get it:

- **Get it donated.** Nearly all major computer companies and software vendors have grant programs for teachers. Check out the corporate Web sites and search for "education" or "teacher."

It's easiest to start out with the local funders. I found it very valuable to be on the site council. I served two terms and learned who the players were. Here, our PTA funds things, our site council funds different things, and then there's an organization called the Palo Alto Foundation for Education. They're very generous to local projects, so there's not so much competition. I started out by learning to do applications to these three groups. And then you start thinking bigger! Every time you have a little success, you think, "OK, who's got the big bucks?" Now we have a partner at Stanford and we're strategizing how to put together a National Science Foundation grant.

—HIGH SCHOOL TEACHER

- Try asking your PTA, other parent groups, or the school site council for the funds you need.
- Ask your principal if discretionary money is available to buy inexpensive software.
- Check out local foundations that donate technology items to schools. National foundations do the same, but the competition is steeper.
- Look for organizations that help companies donate their old computers to schools. Be careful here—you cannot do multimedia projects on computers with old "386" processors.

No matter where you ask, your chances of success are multiplied if you have a coherent plan for using the equipment and can justify technology as essential to your specific teaching goals.

One important caveat: Before you purchase computers or accept donated equipment, find out what your school or district policy is in such cases. Many districts have standards as to platform (for example, Windows or Mac) and minimum requirements. If you get nonstandard equipment, the district may refuse to provide technical support for it. That's a problem you don't need.

All These Multimedia Programs Are New to Me

Given that you do not have to learn all multimedia applications in order to do your first project, what should you learn first? PowerPoint? HyperStudio? GoLive?

In other parts of the book we have discussed choosing applications according to the project you want to do. If this is your first project, the best advice is to find out what application the teacher in the next classroom

> We got a few grants from foundations and listservs. But you have to weigh it. If it takes six hours to write and it's only worth $100, don't do it!
> —ELEMENTARY TEACHER

knows, and use that one. In other words, local support, although not absolutely essential, makes everything so much easier.

Now, given that you do not have to learn your chosen application inside and out, how should you approach the task? There are a few different strategies, depending on how you like to learn.

Find a friend. Many new computer users find people they know and trust to help them through the beginning stages or to solve computer problems and questions. These friends come in many forms—neighborhood children, your school's computer technology teacher, or someone you know who was recently a beginner, too.

Take a class. Many school districts, community colleges, and university continuing education programs offer classes in multimedia applications, Web authoring and design, and the like. These classes range from half- or full-day workshops to semester courses. You can also take classes online through Connected University and other Web sites. The advantages of taking a course include personal help from the teacher and other students, as well as continuing education or course credit. On the other hand, a course does take time.

Attend a conference. There are many conferences for teachers that include workshops on technology. You can attend a one-hour workshop, walk away with lesson plans and reference materials, and then attend a different workshop on another topic the next hour.

Use software tutorials. Most software includes some sort of "getting started" activity or tutorial that guides you step by step through the basics of the program. Spending an hour or two with these tutorials usually gives you most of what you need to know for the average classroom project.

Buy a book. There are many books available, particularly for complex programs like Photoshop. The books are often more comprehensible than the

As far as actual *technical* training, I learn quite well from the Peachpit Press books. I just get one of those and the program I want to learn and then go at it.

—MIDDLE SCHOOL TEACHER

online help or manuals and include all sorts of tips, shortcuts, and examples. Some are even written especially for teachers. You can use them for getting started and then as a reference as you encounter problems during the project.

Do your project. People who are fairly adept at using "help" systems and manuals often prefer to learn by doing. If you try to do the same kind of project as the one you are about to assign, you are bound to run across the same information your students will need, and you will get a feel for what you are really asking of them.

Peripherals generally require the most technical support. It may come from school or district support people, if you have them. If not, plan on spending some time with each peripheral you use, learning how to hook it up, how to import or export media to and from the applications you use, and how to use special features and options.

For example, to use a digital camera for multimedia production, you have to figure out:

- Where to plug it into the computer.
- How to use the camera software to move your photos from the camera to the computer.
- Whether the file format your camera produces is appropriate for the application you are using (for example, is it pict or jpg?) and how to convert files if necessary.

Occasionally everything will go smoothly and everything will work the first time, just like on those TV home repair shows. If you or your closest technical

I'd have an iMac over here and a PowerPC over there. The two wouldn't work together, and yet I didn't anticipate that when I started. All the peripherals, all the adapters I had to buy, was way past anything that I knew was coming. Every time I wanted to hook up a digital camera or a regular camera, I ran into complications.

—ELEMENTARY TEACHER

Equipment is becoming less of a problem. What is still a problem is that there's only one of me. I would like to have parents come in, and I would work with them ahead of time. It would be nice to have the extra help. If I'm over here trouble-shooting, I would like parents to be troubleshooting in the other two places that are probably giving us problems. Parents can also be another person kids can bounce ideas off of.

—MIDDLE SCHOOL TEACHER

One of my most supportive parent friends has spent hundreds of hours putting together last year's video yearbook with his own high-end equipment. This year he came after work on a Friday and hooked up the scan converter that was sitting around my room for months. That enabled me to show the computer screen on the TV for instruction and transfer the students' work to video-tape for sharing. I've wanted to do that for years. He's also given me help over the phone, and his child, one of my youngest students, is a great resource.

—SPECIAL EDUCATION TEACHER

support can't get things working, sometimes a student or parent can help. You can also call the manufacturer.

I'm Worried About Managing the Technology and the Learning at the Same Time

You should be—at least at first. That's why it's so helpful to get your technical support ducks in a row before you start the project. Here are some things you can do to minimize the likelihood that technical problems will derail your project:

Find and train adult volunteers. These might be parents who work in the tech industry or parents who are interested in multimedia. Pre-service teachers from local universities might be interested in gaining experience. You can advertise for volunteers from local technology companies. Teach your volunteers the basics you know, and let them learn on the job like you do. Having more bodies in the room to restart a computer or find supplies will free you for those delicious subject matter discussions you will have with your students.

Get to know your media and technical support people. Explain the project you have in mind and its schedule, and make sure support is available when you need it.

Organize reference materials. Make sure that manuals, books, and supplies are readily available to anyone who wants to work on a problem.

Depend on your students. Many have done projects in other classes or are hobbyists or experts themselves. Even if they start out as beginners, they will all learn different things as they go so that by the end of the project the class as a whole knows a tremendous amount.

Work with another teacher. Find another teacher who wants to do a project similar to yours. Plan the project together and do it at the same time in each of your classrooms. Your partner will become your best friend during the project—you'll want to talk every day about what happened, solve problems together, show each other what your students have done, and share what you have figured out.

School Politics Is Working Against This Kind of Project

You return from a technology conference flush with excitement about the multimedia project you want to do. And all anyone wants to know is how many textbook pages behind you will be at the end of the project. At best they all think you're nuts; at worst they accuse you of bringing down the whole school's test scores for your own selfish pleasure.

This is not something to be taken lightly, and if this is the kind of school you teach in, you should not feel guilty for making some compromises. You may be able to do it all, but not right away.

Some of our teachers began in schools that were very successful with traditional instructional practices. Teachers who wanted to do projects had to start very small. Five or six years and many small steps later, many schools came to see the value of technology. Our teachers built bridges to individuals by finding small pieces of project-based multimedia learning that corresponded to accepted practices such as using a rubric or using a process approach. Once they formed a small community of advocates, they began collecting data, showing how multimedia projects promoted consistent

My close network helps me first—I go to my Web person, my screwdriver person.

—ELEMENTARY TEACHER

There are lots of resources right there in the room. Kids are a great resource. Just say to them, "Here's our problem—does anyone know how to get around it?"

—TECHNOLOGY LEARNING
COORDINATOR

The practice of curricular change includes a hefty dose of politics. Any number of committees need to feel involved.

—TECHNOLOGY LEARNING
COORDINATOR

Our strategy was to begin to talk about the *elements* of project-based learning without using the dreaded p-word. We began to build a cycle of reflection and practice based on changing the language. There were words we avoided for two years. We talked about rubric assessment because a lot of people were already using that. The Advanced Placement exams had been using rubrics for years, so that wasn't a stretch. We developed a technology competence rubric based on one that Apple had developed. Another thing was the value of student exhibitions. Fine Arts and Social Studies people understood how important they were. Technology was the hardest sell. There the method was to say, "Those of you who want to do it, hop on board. We won't harass the rest of you." We got a lot more takers than if we'd said, "We're all going there now at the same time."

—HIGH SCHOOL TEACHER

achievement on the district's own standards. They used their data to advocate for systemwide support—and got it.

So what kind of systemwide support systems are helpful, particularly beyond pure technical support? The next chapter describes some systemwide support techniques we developed in the Challenge 2000 Multimedia Project.

9
Building Systemic Support

The Challenge 2000 Multimedia Project was an effort to help teachers become proficient in using the project-based multimedia learning model. It reached 50 schools in the greater Silicon Valley area of California. Here we will sketch out key elements of the Project's approach to capacity building.

The project sponsored a variety of professional development activities for its cadre of teachers. From the beginning, the project adhered to a philosophy of growing grassroots expertise and encouraging teacher-to-teacher learning. Professional development activities were planned and implemented almost entirely by teachers and technology learning coordinators (TLCs)—teachers on leave to provide technology and curriculum support to cadre teachers. These activities include teacher work days, summer institutes, dinner meetings with guest speakers, technology training days, and other activities based on needs of smaller groups of teachers.

Multimedia projects, with all their rewards, *are* a lot of work, and the first time is the hardest. What kind of support makes a teacher take that leap? Because membership in the cadre was always voluntary, this was one of our central questions. Five of our programs had a particularly significant effect on the number of teachers we were able to recruit, as well as on the number of teachers who completed successful projects year after year. These programs were as follows:

- **Technology learning coordinators (TLCs).** A system of teacher leadership for providing support and training.
- **Mini grants.** Project teachers could apply to the project for small grants for equipment and software.
- **Project-Based teacher partnerships.** Inexperienced teachers teamed with an experienced teacher to do a project together.
- **Multimedia fairs.** All of our teachers exhibited projects in district or school-wide multimedia fairs at the end of each academic year.
- **Student interviews.** Each district team chose six of its best projects, and the students who created them participated in interviews with a panel of adult experts. The experts rated the projects using the Multimedia Project Rubric (Figure 9.1).

TLCs: Support and Advocacy

The project organized and supported a network of teachers on leave from part or all of their teaching duties. These teachers, called TLCs, were responsible for recruiting and supporting teachers. Each TLC supported between 3 and 18 teachers at their own school and others in their districts. They were released from their teaching duties—anywhere from one period per day to full time—and paid their regular salary. The TLC's main responsibilities were:

During the school day I'm a Swiss army knife with an identity crisis.
—TECHNOLOGY LEARNING COORDINATOR

FIGURE 9.1 MULTIMEDIA PROJECT RUBRIC

Multimedia Project Scoring Rubric

Score Levels	**Multimedia** *The integration of media objects such as text, graphics, video, animation, and sound to represent and convey information. Videotapes which include sound and images fit this definition.*	**Collaboration** *Working together to accomplish a common intellectual purpose in a manner superior to what might have been accomplished working alone.*	**Content** *The topics, ideas, concepts, knowledge, and opinions that constitute the substance of the presentation.*
5	Students have used multimedia in creative and effective ways that exploit the particular strengths of the chosen format. All elements make a contribution. There are few technical problems, and none of a serious nature.	Students were a very effective team. Division of responsibilities capitalized on the strengths of each team member. The final product was shaped by all members and represents something that would not have been possible to accomplish working alone.	Meets all criteria of the previous level and one or more of the following: reflects broad research and application of critical thinking skills; shows notable insight or understanding of the topic; compels the audience's attention.
4	Presentation blends 3 or more multimedia elements in a balanced, attractive, easy-to-follow format. Elements include original student work. With minor exceptions, all elements contribute to, rather than detract from, the presentation's overall effectiveness.	Students worked together as a team on all aspects of the project. There was an effort to assign roles based on the skills/talents of individual members. All members strove to fulfill their responsibilities.	The project has a clear goal related to a significant topic or issue. Information included has been compiled from several relevant sources. The project is useful to an audience beyond the students who created it.
3	Presentation uses 2 or more media. There are some technical problems, but the viewer is able to follow the presentation with few difficulties.	Students worked together on the project as a team with defined roles to play. Most members fulfilled their responsibilities. Disagreements were resolved or managed productively.	The project presents information in an accurate and organized manner that can be understood by the intended audience. There is a focus that is maintained throughout the piece.
2	Presentation uses 2 or more media, but technical difficulties seriously interfere with the viewer's ability to see, hear, or understand content.	Presentation is the result of a group effort, but only some members of the group contributed. There is evidence of poor communication, unresolved conflict, or failure to collaborate on important aspects of the work.	The project has a focus but may stray from it at times. There is an organizational structure, though it may not be carried through consistently. There may be factual errors or inconsistencies, but they are relatively minor.
1	Multimedia is absent from the presentation.	Presentation was created by one student working more or less alone (though may have received guidance or help from others).	Project seems haphazard, hurried, or unfinished. There are significant factual errors, misconceptions, or misunderstandings.
	Multimedia score =	**Collaboration score =**	**Content score =**

Project Title: _____ Grade _____ Date _____ Judge's initials _____

Directions: Give the project a 1, 2, 3, 4, or 5 in each category.

Source: San Mateo (California) County Office of Education, 2001. Reproduced by permission.

I wanted to offer training for the nine cadre members, and I knew we'd have to do it after school. I thought that since the lab has 30 computers, we would just open it up to everyone. And it turned out that many of the cadre teachers helped the others learn.

—TECHNOLOGY LEARNING
COORDINATOR

Having the TLC there made all the difference—someone to talk about *education* and guide the students through.

—TECHNOLOGY LEARNING
COORDINATOR

• Design, organize, and provide training, coaching and other support to assist project cadre teachers with the design and implementation of exemplary project-based multimedia learning, as defined by the Challenge 2000 Multimedia Project.

• Attend and support monthly TLC professional development meetings.

• Coordinate an annual exhibition of student multimedia projects.

• Provide initial on-site technical support to cadre teachers, if needed, for the use of multimedia software and network tools.

• Serve as a coach to support the integration of technology into instructional programs throughout the TLC's home school and district.

• Assist with planning, coordination, and implementation of project-wide professional development activities.

It turned out that the presence of the TLC was often the push a teacher needed to start using technology and to keep using it. Without a TLC, technology use lost momentum and faltered. Why did the program work so well? Here are some lessons we learned along the way.

Support needs to be more than technical. The topics in this book make it is easy to see that technical assistance is a small (though necessary) part of making a multimedia project successful. Teaching and learning issues are complex and intertwined with technical concerns. The ideal teacher support should come from someone who can not only show teachers how to hook up the scanner but can suggest ways to organize the scanning process to maximize student learning and engagement. We firmly believe that it is far easier to teach teachers about technology than it is to teach technicians about education, which is why TLCs had to be teachers first.

Many of our districts had technical support for necessary things like hooking up a network and maintaining equipment. But in addition to pure technical support, you need technology-related *instructional* support.

"Find your rabbits and run with them." All of the TLCs were interested in technology before the Challenge 2000 Multimedia Project came along. Many were *passionate* about it. Not just because it was fun but because they saw the changes it brought about in their classrooms and how it engaged students they had never engaged before. They didn't serve the project; they *used and learned from it* to help them with a mission they already had. They were happy to get the release period—it allowed them to do the work they would have done anyway and to get paid for it instead of burning out. There are probably people like these TLCs in your district, and if you find them and let them work together, nothing will stop them.

The job doesn't have to be full time. Some TLCs did the job full time. Others were released from just one or two periods per day and supported fewer teachers and schools. Elementary school teachers tended to be full time, because it is so much harder for an elementary school teacher to do a part-time job. A middle or high school teacher has a more segmented day to portion out.

There were advantages and disadvantages to part- and full-time versions of the job. The part-timers enjoyed the credibility that comes with doing a project in their own classrooms concurrent with their TLC duties. The disadvantage was that they were always faced with balancing the demands of their own teaching with their duties as TLCs. Furthermore, part-timers sometimes had trouble providing adequate instructional support because the school pulled them away to provide technical support. Full-timers could focus all their attention on their TLC roles and manage their schedules without

I do think that *teacher-helping-teacher* is a much stronger model than *some outside person-helping-teacher.* Now it might work if you had some outside person with a lot of credibility already in place and you wanted to give them this extra TLC anointment. But I'd rather have somebody that's in the classroom and has tried this stuff with their students.

—TECHNOLOGY LEARNING
COORDINATOR

Before there were computers, I was the person who could thread the film projector.

—TECHNOLOGY LEARNING
COORDINATOR

All the TLCs in this project had technology as a hobby to start with; that's what gets them through the frustrations. They'd be doing it anyway, if not in the school environment then they'd be going home and putting their Web pages together.

—TECHNOLOGY LEARNING
COORDINATOR

The positive of being both a TLC and a teacher is that you're talking to teachers as a fellow teacher—not *at* them but *with* them. They know that I understand how hard kids can be or how hard it is to work with the schedules or when the technology fails. I knew all of these things because they happened to me. The hard part is the time it takes.

—TECHNOLOGY LEARNING
COORDINATOR

Transformation of education is not a training issue but a feedback cycle.

—TECHNOLOGY LEARNING
COORDINATOR

People learn faster because of ongoing on-site support from the TLC. I don't just do a workshop and walk away, leaving them to figure it out on their own. They have someone there beside them, getting them to open up to new perspectives.

—TECHNOLOGY LEARNING
COORDINATOR

worrying about being back for their 3rd period classes. They were freer to help out in another teacher's classroom. They could spend a whole day debugging a problem if they had to.

On site is best. Most of the TLCs supported teachers at their own schools and at least one other school. There was general agreement among the TLCs that they were more effective in their home schools. First, people already knew them and credibility was less of a problem. Teachers could catch them in the halls with quick questions. They could take five minutes between class periods to fix a problem. Teachers new to technology feel much more willing to take risks if they know they can get help within minutes, rather than hours or days.

Networking is crucial. The TLCs met formally every month. Some TLCs also met monthly with TLCs from their own district. Once they all got to know each other, they frequently phoned or e-mailed each other with questions, or got together to learn a new piece of software or to develop training materials. Nearly all the TLCs came to depend on this network—their collective brain held the answers to nearly every conceivable question. The monthly meetings were opportunities for professional development activities and project business, but most importantly they were opportunities for sharing ideas and collaborative problem solving.

Take advantage of the rhythms of the school year. The Challenge 2000 Multimedia Project had a regular flow of events throughout the school year that provided a structure for the TLCs to work with. The months September through November were occupied with training, planning, and preparing project grant applications. In the middle of the year, TLCs supported teachers in their classrooms. April was for multimedia fairs and project judging. May and June were for archiving projects and evaluating the year. This structure meant that everyone was doing the same thing at more or less the same time, making it easier to focus TLC meetings and provide assistance to TLCs and teachers.

In summary, if you want to unleash a powerful force in your district, find the teachers who are passionate about technology, give them some time and money, let them do the job on a schedule that makes sense for them, have a TLC on every school site, and get them together every month until they turn into a community. Then continue to change and grow the TLC support program to meet the needs of your school's increasing technical prowess.

Mini Grants: A Local Grant Program

Each year, a pool of money was set aside for small grants. These grants could be used to buy specialized equipment or software for particular projects, such as scanners, digital cameras, or photoediting software. Teachers could apply for up to $2000 to support their projects.

Although we did this as part of the Challenge 2000 Multimedia Project, a school district could have a similar program. The mini grant program actually served three purposes: giving financial support to projects, supporting teachers' planning processes, and motivating teachers to join the project, if only for the free stuff. The application form required the following:

- Title of project.
- Names of lead teacher and partners and their grade levels/subject areas.
- Number of students contributing to the multimedia product(s).
- An abstract of two or three sentences that included both the content of the project and the type of multimedia product students would produce.

> Having a TLC there on site brought the buy-in way up—at my school the whole 3rd and 5th grades are participating. It's harder at the other schools I support. The teachers don't know me. They have to call me to come over when they have a problem.
> — TECHNOLOGY LEARNING COORDINATOR

> I wouldn't miss TLC meetings. I like the networking, discussing what others are doing, and the self assessment—how am I doing compared to the group?
> —TECHNOLOGY LEARNING COORDINATOR

> We TLCs always yak yak yak about how do you do this and that.
> —TECHNOLOGY LEARNING COORDINATOR

- The three main instructional goals of the project (to be drawn from the California State Content Standards, frameworks, or local district curriculum).
- A concrete, measurable objective for each of the three instructional goals.
- A description of how to determine if one of the objectives was met.
- A description of the final multimedia product and its elements (for example, sounds, pictures, animations, text, and so forth).
- A description of the forms of collaboration represented in the project.
- A description of the kinds of decisions students would make in the course of the project.
- A description of the real-world connection(s) in the project.
- A project calendar showing key project milestones.

As you can see, this application form, although brief, required teachers to think through all seven dimensions of the model. TLCs and project staff evaluated each application and gave constructive feedback designed to increase the teacher's probability of success. Nearly all applications were ultimately funded, and many applicants commented that their projects were stronger for having gone through the application process.

Project-Based Teacher Partnerships

The purpose of the partnerships program was to significantly increase the number of teachers participating in the project. TLCs and project staff developed the program to take advantage of the significant expertise that had grown and to encourage all experienced teachers to spread the model to

> I guess I was just so intrigued with free equipment that *that* was the lure that got me to gamble. I thought I could do this once. I couldn't see beyond this year. I thought, OK, if it fails, fine. I've got the experience now, I've got the equipment in my room, I can do something else with it. Now I know for a fact it will be used year after year for multimedia until it dies.
>
> —ELEMENTARY TEACHER

other teachers at their school. Thus the program served a dual function of recruitment and professional development.

Teachers who had already used the model (called lead teachers) formed partnerships with one or more other teachers in their schools. They then planned a project that each partner implemented in her classroom. Participating teachers received a $500 stipend for completing the project, and partnerships were eligible for the mini grants described above. To participate, teachers had to submit a detailed plan for the project-based unit that they would do together.

Lead teachers received an extra stipend for supporting their partners and helping them learn the necessary technology. At the end of the project, all teachers had to complete a survey and submit completed student multimedia projects.

The model owes its success to many factors. The following seemed especially significant:

- **The application process.** Preparing the project proposal lent a formality to the arrangement and encouraged detailed planning. Furthermore, going through the application process made teachers ready when approval came, and meetings could focus on the day-to-day planning rather than on questions of what the project should be.
- **Focus on a project.** The demands of the project itself structured partnership meetings and kept them productive. Teachers were operating in the context of an ongoing unit. Partners would decide together what they were going to do tomorrow, and then they'd go do it. The focus on a project also meant that the partnership was over when the project was over. Teachers didn't feel they had signed on for life, so recruitment was easier.

• **Self-selected, voluntary local partners.** Teachers selected their own partners and tended to select teachers they had worked with before or were friendly with. Having partners within the school made response easy because they met in the halls or the teachers' lounge.

• **Flexibility.** Participants were free to decide what they needed and how to support one another. Partners most often met through impromptu encounters rather than scheduled meetings. When they met, they discussed technology issues, looked at student work, planned activities, and shared strategies.

• **Multimedia fairs.** The project held a series of multimedia fairs at the end of the year that were open to the public. As part of their agreement with the project, partnership teachers were expected to exhibit their students' multimedia work. The approaching deadlines helped teachers give projects an ending point that also mattered to students. It led to another round of collaboration among partnership teachers as they worked to consolidate student projects and to get everyone ready for the fair.

Multimedia Fairs

Annual exhibitions of student multimedia projects were a key feature of the project. Held each year as a culminating activity, these public exhibitions served to motivate project completion and reward teachers and students for their accomplishments. Each school team held its own exhibition, typically in a large multipurpose room. Scores of computers, monitors, projectors, and other equipment were moved into the room. Students and teachers manned their particular stations and proudly demonstrated their multimedia projects. As rooms filled with parents, administrators, school board members, and interested members of the public, a spirited, carnival atmosphere prevailed.

The multimedia fairs were wonderful. I loved it—I had two school districts, and they don't usually work together. So I purposely had them come together in the same auditorium and share. Very exciting. Parents and kids are so excited about what they've learned, and what they have learned is so significant. People were amazed, even at things like 2nd graders reading at the level they could. It was phenomenal.

—TECHNOLOGY LEARNING
COORDINATOR

Sometimes local reporters covered the event and local politicians gave welcome speeches.

Schools experimented with the fairs over the years, changing the size, the format, or the focus. Everyone agreed that big fairs with lots of participating schools are powerful for engaging the community and building support for multimedia. They are exciting for students, too. But they are so much work to put together that many moved to a smaller, one-school format. Several fairs successfully piggybacked on open house night or another existing event. Teachers and students could show off projects without having to move computers and multimedia files to another location, and organizers didn't have to do separate publicity and logistical work.

Instead of setting up tables around the room, schools allowed each group of students five minutes to demonstrate their project to the whole audience on a large-screen TV. Each project had its moment in the sun, and audience members could see the projects better than they could on small computer screens.

As projects grew stronger in real-world connection, some schools were able to exhibit in a way that made sense for the themes of the projects. For example, in one school all projects had a drug abuse prevention theme, and the school held a Drug Abuse Resistance Education (DARE) fair that featured the projects.

Student Interviews

Student interviews were held around the same time as the fairs. Unlike the noisy, frenetic exhibitions, these interviews afforded a protected and focused opportunity to get an in-depth look at a selected sample of student multimedia projects. By scoring the students' work with the Multimedia Project Rubric, the project could gather data over time on the quality of the work being done.

Judges reported to the interview site first thing in the morning. During a continental breakfast, judges received orientation and training in the use of the rubric from a project staff member who served as facilitator. This was followed by a series of 30-minute interviews. At each interview, the student authors shared their multimedia project with the judges and answered questions designed to elicit the information necessary to score the project. After students departed, judges completed their score sheets independently. Next, scores were mapped on chart paper or a chalkboard. With the guidance of the facilitator, the judges discussed any large scoring discrepancies. Judges stated the reasons for their scores and cited evidence from the students' project or comments. Typically, the discussion resulted in some judges revising their scores up or down.

Each project team of schools selected six of their best projects for scoring—essentially creating a *team portfolio* that represented a wide range of grade levels. Why six? With 30 minutes for the interview itself and another 30 minutes for the judges to score, discuss, and resolve discrepancies, it required a full hour to evaluate and rate a single project. Even working through lunch, staff found that six is the maximum number of interviews that can be completed in a day.

By using the same rubric and process year after year, the project staff got a sense of how projects were changing and improving. TLCs used their team's scores to focus their training for next year: was content weak overall? Did teachers need help designing collaborative projects? (See figure 9.1 on page 119 for sample rubric.)

The projects this year were a huge jump in technology. We looked at our scores from last year, analyzing why they weren't all "4." For a lot of them, it was because the multimedia just wasn't so exciting.

—TECHNOLOGY LEARNING
COORDINATOR

Synergy: TLCs, Partnerships, Mini Grants, Fairs, and Interviews

These five programs each helped the Challenge 2000 Multimedia Project achieve its goals, and each could be replicated individually. Our experience was that doing them all allowed us to leverage the power of each to make the others easier and more effective.

TLCs were central to the success of each of the other programs. They helped organize and support partnerships. They assisted teachers in preparing mini grant applications and worked together to coordinate efforts to improve them. They organized the multimedia fairs and student interviews and selected the six projects for their teams' portfolios. The programs helped the TLCs, too. It gave a rhythm to their year and a focus for their work. In the fall they helped with mini grants and partnerships. In the later part of the year everyone had the multimedia fairs and interviews in mind as they polished projects, thought through selection for the interviews, and scrambled to finish on time.

Partnerships were closely related to the mini grant program. Most partnerships applied for mini grants and used the process to help them focus their planning. Part of the requirement for mini grants and partnership stipends was that the teachers' students had to participate in the multimedia fair.

You can probably discover other kinds of synergy in your own district that result from having multiple programs work together. For us, it was natural that as we created each new program, we would use the resources we had already created to make the new program successful.

Glossary

Application: Software designed for the "end-user" (the person who uses software to do a task). Examples include word processors, drawing programs, and image editors. Contrast with operating system.

Authoring: Creating multimedia.

Authoring programs: Applications that help you assemble multimedia presentations.

Browser: Software for viewing pages on the Internet. Examples include Netscape Navigator and Internet Explorer.

Bookmark: A record of the URL of a Web site. Some browsers call these "favorites."

Collaboration: Working together to accomplish a common intellectual purpose in a manner superior to what might have been accomplished working alone.

Dimensions of project-based multimedia learning: Seven aspects that together make an exemplary unit. The dimensions are assessment, collaboration, content, extended time frame, multimedia, real-world connection, and student decision making.

Flowchart: A series of symbols that show how a multimedia presentation will flow. Typically, each screen is symbolized by a simple box with the title of the screen. Decisions made by the user are symbolized by diamond boxes, and arrow lines between the boxes and the diamonds show where in the presentation the user will go next.

Hardware: Computer and peripheral devices. Contrast with **software**, the programs that run on those devices.

Home page: The main page of a Web site from which a user can access all the other pages.

Hypermedia: A computer- or Web-based presentation in which the user navigates through information by clicking on text or images.

Hyperlink: Clickable image or text in a multimedia presentation that takes the user to a different part of the presentation. Also called a *link*.

HTML: Hypertext Markup Language. A language for formatting Web pages. Web authoring programs generate HTML automatically for simple pages; users can write HTML for more complicated pages.

Image: A picture or graphic in digital format.

Media object: A unit of text, graphics, sound, motion, or interactivity.

Multimedia: The integration of media objects such as text, graphics, video, animation, and sound to represent and convey information.

Operating system: The programs that make the computer do basic tasks like boot up, run **applications**, and communicate with **peripherals**. Examples include Mac OS and Microsoft Windows.

Peripheral: Equipment that connects to a computer to move media in or out of the computer. Examples include scanners, digital cameras, microphones, and printers.

Project-based learning: A teaching method in which students acquire new knowledge and skills in the course of designing, planning, and producing some product or performance.

Project-based multimedia learning: A method of teaching in which students acquire new knowledge and skills in the course of designing, planning, and producing a multimedia product.

Scanner: A peripheral that translates a picture on paper to digital format.

Software: The programs that run on a computer.

Stand-alone presentation: A multimedia product that can be used on a single computer without either human assistance or an Internet connection.

Storyboard: A series of sketches of media screens that will comprise a presentation. Making a storyboard is a good way to plan the content and hyperlinks for a presentation before doing time-consuming media production.

URL (Uniform Resource Locator): A standard "address" for Web pages. For example, the URL for ASCD is http://www.ascd.org.

Universal file format: A file format that can be understood by many different programs. Examples include jpg, pict, and gif. Converting media to universal formats makes it easy to move it from one program to another.

Web page: A document on the World Wide Web. Each Web page is identified by a unique address called a URL.

Web site: One or more related documents, or Web pages, on the World Wide Web.

References and Resources

References

Copyright and fair use (http://fairuse.Stanford.edu). (2002). Stanford University.

Fenstermacher, G. D., & Soltis, J. F. (1998). *Approaches to teaching.* New York: Teachers College Press.

Glasser, W. (1975). *Schools without failure.* New York: HarperCollins/ Perennial.

Joyce, B. R., & Weil, M. (2000). *Models of teaching* (6th ed.). Boston: Allyn & Bacon.

Lynch, P. J., & Horton, S. (1999). *Web style guide: Basic design principles for creating Web sites.* New Haven: Yale University Press.

Murnane, R. J. & Levy, F. (1996). *Teaching the new basic skills: Principles for educating children to thrive in a changing economy.* New York: Free Press.

Penuel, W. R., Means, B., & Simkins, M. (2000, October). The multimedia challenge. *Educational Leadership, 58*(2), 34–38.

Popham, W. J. (1998). *Classroom assessment: What teachers need to know.* Boston: Allyn & Bacon.

The Secretary's Commission on Achieving Necessary Skills. (1991). *What work requires of schools: A SCANS report for America 2000.* Washington, DC: U.S. Department of Labor.

Williams, R., & Tollett, J. (2000). *The non-designer's Web book.* Berkeley: Peachpit Press.

Other Resources

Connected University is an online professional development community providing educators with courses, resources, and support. By subscription http://cu.classroom.com.

The *George Lucas Educational Foundation* spotlights classrooms where innovations such as project-based learning and new digital multimedia are taking place in hopes of encouraging change in other schools. http://www.glef.org

Multimedia: A sneak preview is a 15-minute video to show to students before beginning project work; available online from WestEd, http://www.wested.org/cs/wew/view/rs/609.

Looking at Student Work presents the work of educators who have created guidelines for new ways of looking at student work. http://www.lasw.org

The *Project-Based Learning with Multimedia* CD-ROM includes stories, interviews, templates, and a project planning tool. It's available from ASCD's online store, http://shop.ascd.org/ProductDisplay. cfm?ProductID=502117

The *Project-Based Learning with Multimedia* Web site had many additional classroom resources, research reports, and a public database where teachers can share project plans with one another. http://pblmm.k12.ca.us

The *WEB Project* is a non-profit organization devoted to innovative, project-based learning in the arts, humanities, and social sciences by people of all ages. http://www.webproject.org

Index

Note: Page numbers followed by *f* indicate figures.

About the Authors

The authors are leaders from the *Challenge 2000 Multimedia Project* and the *WEB Project*, two award-winning federally funded technology projects for teachers and students in grades kindergarten through 12.

Michael Simkins is creative director of Portical.org, a Web portal commissioned by the State of California to support California's 25,000 K–12 school administrators as technology leaders. Previously, he was director of technology initiatives at Joint Venture: Silicon Valley Network, where his responsibilities included directing the Challenge 2000 Multimedia Project. Simkins's career includes 15 years in the classroom as an elementary school teacher and 9 years as an elementary principal. He holds a master's degree in teacher education and a doctorate in curriculum. His articles have appeared in *Educational Leadership, Technology and Learning,* and *Principal.* He regularly presents workshops at state and national educational technology conferences. Contact Simkins at P.O. Box 6361, Los Osos, CA 93412; phone: (408) 482-9492; fax: (805) 528-0246; e-mail: mbsimkins@charter.net.

Karen Cole is a senior research associate at WestEd, a nonprofit research, development, and service agency with headquarters in San Francisco. Prior to that, she was a research scientist at the Institute for Research on Learning (IRL). A 20-year veteran in the educational technology field, she has worked in research, curriculum development, assessment development, evaluation, and teacher professional development. Her award-winning projects include the *Middle School Math through Applications Project* curriculum and the CD-ROM *A Video Exploration of Classroom Assessment.* Contact Cole at P.O. Box 27, Garrett Park, MD 20896; e-mail: kac@karencole.com.

Fern Tavalin is the executive director of the WEB Project, Inc. (http://www.webproject.org). She was one of the prime conceivers and developers of the federal technology innovation grant The WEB Project: Creating a WEB of Evidence. Tavalin specializes in project-based learning, using collaborative inquiry as a process for improvement, and offers experientially based summer multimedia institutes to teachers. Her concepts about educational technology and applied learning have been formally translated into a pragmatic design called

Applied Learning Studios (http://www.appliedlearning.org). She also specializes in developing systems of collaborative online inquiry. Contact Tavalin at 270 Putney Mountain Road, Putney, VT 05346; phone: (802) 387-4277; e-mail: tavalin@ sover.net.

Barbara Means directs the Center for Technology in Learning at SRI International, an independent non-profit research organization based in Menlo Park, California. Means collaborated on the original design of the *Challenge 2000 Multimedia Project* and supervised its evaluation activities. She has directed numerous research projects concerned with the design, implementation, and evaluation of technology-enhanced approaches to education reform. Her recent work includes case studies of technology use in urban high schools, published as *The Connected School*. Her earlier published works include the edited volumes *Technology and Education Reform* and *Teaching Advanced Skills to At-Risk Students*. Contact Means at SRI International, 333 Ravenswood Avenue, Menlo Park, CA 94025; phone: (650) 859-4004; e-mail: barbara.means@sri.com.

●   ●   ●

In the *Challenge 2000 Multimedia Project,* a cadre of 140 teachers from 50 schools in the greater Silicon Valley area of California worked for more than five years with consultants from the Institute for Research on Learning, WestEd, and SRI International to develop best practices in the use of multimedia presentation programs within a project-based learning context.

The *WEB Project* is now a nonprofit organization devoted to developing innovative uses of technology for collaborative learning in the arts, humanities, and social sciences by people of all ages. *The WEB Project* has developed many effective strategies and assessment tools that influence practices throughout Vermont and across the United States.

In the year 2000, the *Challenge 2000 Multimedia Project* was one of only two programs to receive the "Exemplary Educational Technology Program" designation from the U.S. Department of Education, and the *WEB Project* was one of only five projects to receive the designation of "Promising Educational Technology Program."

Multimedia: A Sneak Preview, by Karen Cole and Michael Simkins, is a video on project-based learning with multimedia, available from WestEd (http://www.wested.org/cs/wew/view/rs/609). The video describes what kids have to say about projects they undertook at Silicon Valley elementary, middle, and high school classrooms in the nationally acclaimed *Challenge 2000 Multimedia Project.*

The students share six stages of planning, designing, and producing curriculum-based classroom multimedia projects. The video is specially designed for classroom teachers to show to students when they first embark on their projects. It also serves as a quick overview of this teaching approach for parents, administrators, and community members. Additional ideas for using the video can be found on the project-based learning with multimedia Web site.

See the ASCD Web site (http://www.ascd.org/) and go to the Online Store for information about the CD-ROM *Project-Based Learning with Multimedia* and other resources on project-based learning and technology in education.

Related ASCD Resources:
Project-Based Learning and Multimedia

Audiotapes

Differentiation for the 21st Century: Technology as a Teaching Tool, by Linda Brandon and Sally Simon (#201206)

The Internet and Brain-Based Learning: A Powerful Team, by Kim Lindley and Kristen Nelson (#201128)

Using Technology Raises Student Test Scores, by Ted Ammann and Susan Giancola (#201122)

CD-ROMs and Multimedia

Educational Leadership on CD-ROM, 1992–98 (1 hybrid CD-ROM) (#598223)

Problem-Based Learning Across the Curriculum Professional Development Kit by Shelagh Gallagher and Bill Stepien (#997148)

Project-Based Learning with Multimedia by the San Mateo County Office of Education (1 hybrid CD-ROM) (#502117)

The Research on Technology for Learning CD-ROM by North Central Regional Educational Laboratory (1 hybrid CD-ROM) (#597001)

Networks

Visit the ASCD Web site (www.ascd.org) and search for "networks" for information about professional educators who have formed groups around topics like "Authentic Assessment," "Information Literacy," "Integrating Technology in the Elementary Classroom," "Online Learning Network: Learning on the Internet," "Problem-Based Learning," and "Technology in the Middle School." Look in the "Network Directory" for current facilitators' addresses and phone numbers.

Online Resources

Visit ASCD's Web site (www.ascd.org) for the following professional development opportunities on online articles:

"Copyright 101" by Carol Simpson, in *Educational Leadership,* 59(4), December 2001/January 2002 (Available online: http://www.ascd.org/readingroom/edlead/0112/simpson.html).

Online Tutorials, such as *The Brain and Learning* and *Problem-based Learning* (http://www.ascd.org/frametutorials. html) (free).

Professional Development Online: *Only the Best—Evaluating Software and Internet Resources,* by Jamie Sawatsky, Kathy Checkley,

and Mary Beth Neilson; and *Planning for Technology,* by Vicki Hancock (http://www.ascd.org/framepdonline.html) (for a small fee; password protected).

"The Project Approach to Learning" by Rick Allen, in *Curriculum Update,* Spring 2001 (Available online: http://www.ascd.org/readingroom/cupdate/2001/allen2.html).

"Teaching and Learning with Presentation Software" by Susan Lafond, in *Curriculum/Technology Quarterly,* 9(10), Fall 1999 (Available online: http://www.ascd.org/readingroom/ctq/vol09/1fall.html).

Print Products

Educational Leadership: Teaching the Information Generation (Vol. 58, No. 2, October 2000) (#100284)

The New Basics: Education and the Future of Work in the Telematic Age by David Thornburg (#102005)

Teaching Every Student in the Digital Age: Universal Design for Learning by David Rose and Anne Meyer (#101042)

Teaching Middle School Students to Be Active Researchers by Judith M. Zorfass with Harriet Copel (#198180)

Using the Internet to Strengthen Curriculum by Larry Lewin (#100042)

Visual Literacy: Learn to See, See to Learn by Lynell Burmark (#101226)

Visual Tools for Constructing Knowledge by David Hyerle (#196072)

Videotapes

Educating Everybody's Children. Tape 4: Increasing Interest, Motivation, and Engagement (#400225)

Helping Students Acquire and Integrate Knowledge Series (5 tapes, part of the Dimensions of Learning program) (#496065)

Teaching and Learning with New Technologies: Teaching and Learning with the Internet: 2 Videos (#496047)

The Lesson Collection. Tape 14: Environmental Project—Internet (Middle School) (#400066)

For additional information, visit us on the World Wide Web (http://www.ascd.org), send an e-mail message to member@ascd.org, call the ASCD Service Center (1-800-933-ASCD or 703-578-9600, then press 2), send a fax to 703-575-5400, or write to Information Services, ASCD, 1703 N. Beauregard St., Alexandria, VA 22311-1714 USA.